Southern Utah's Desert Outpost

Making Peace with the Past, Pursuing Peace in the Present

St. George, Utah
September 12–15, 2024

John Whitmer Historical Association

Presidential Welcome

I have eagerly anticipated this year's conference in St. George, Utah. This conference has been in the works for more than five years, having been postponed due to Covid in 2020, and will be our first conference west of the Missouri River. Mark Staker and Rachel Killebrew, program chairs, have worked tirelessly to put together an exceptional conference. Here we will explore southern Utah's desert outpost, with exciting tours and presentations planned to orient you to the region's meaningful Restoration history. We also hope you will take the time to explore the area's beautiful "Color Country," including Zion National Park while you are in the area.

I really enjoyed last year's conference where we learned more about the Wightite communities who braved difficult conditions for years in the Texas Hill Country. Next year, we once again return to the more familiar Restoration sites near Independence, Missouri. Wherever we gather from year to year, it is always a pleasure to reunite with friends who have a common interest in Restoration history. These connections are as meaningful to me as the scholarship we will enjoy. We will have many first-time attendees this year at our conference, and I encourage you to get to know someone new and welcome them into our Restoration family. I trust that you have a memorable and enlightening experience during our conference this year!

Kyle R. Walker, JWHA President

JWHA celebrates diversity and is committed to creating an inclusive environment for our members and attendees. We encourage participants to keep their minds open to new perspectives as they respectfully listen and share with one another.

The conference center is a smoke-and-pet-free venue.

To ensure a safe conference for all attendees, JWHA practices weapons-free events.

Covid Precautions: Again, this year we will be mindful of keeping our guests safe and recommend attendees consider wearing masks for their personal safety. If you're not feeling well, please consider self-quarantine.

Sponsors

Thank you to our generous awards sponsors:

Smith-Pettit Foundation
Dan and Beth Whittemore
Greg and Cynthia Kofford
Jerry Mogg
Joe Geisner
Katherine Pollock

Cover painting by Maynard Dixon

Name Tags

Please wear your name tag throughout the conference. Your name tag is your registration confirmation and ticket to attend additional agenda items you have registered for. Those agenda items are noted at the bottom of your nametag. Check the Agenda at a Glance for times and locations.

WD1 – Friday Night Downtown Walking Tour – Group 1
WD2 – Friday Night Downtown Walking Tour – Group 2
WB – Friday Night Juanita Brooks Walking Tour
SC – Saturday Afternoon Short Creek Bus Tour
MM – Saturday Afternoon Mountain Meadows Bus Tour
P – Presidential Address & Banquet

Single-day registration will be indicated by the registered day.

Your silent auction bid number is on the back of your name tag.

Door Prize Drawing

There will be three door prize drawings during the conference. You received a ticket in your name tag. Retain the "Keep This Coupon" ticket, then listen for your number to be called.

Want to increase your chances and support our fundraising? Additional tickets are available at registration, five for $10 or $3 each.

You must be present to win.

John Whitmer
Historical Association Auction

Silent Auction:

The silent auction that takes place each year at the JWHA annual conference is a popular tradition. It is fun for conference attenders, and it raises funds for the John Whitmer Historical Association. There are always items of interest and value on the auction tables. You will find your silent auction number on the back of your name tag to bid on items throughout the conference. The bidding will end on Saturday, September 14, at Noon. Items won must be paid for when picked up at the conference after the auction closes. Take some time between conference sessions to see the items on the auction tables. Thanks to all those who generously donated items for our auctions. And thanks to those who participate in the bidding.

Where Your Conference $$$ Go

2024 JWHA Officers & Staff

Executive Committee		
	President	Kyle Walker
	President Elect	Mark Staker
	Immediate Past President	Casey Griffiths
	Executive Director	Cheryle Grinter
	Treasurer	Robert Cook
Board of Directors		
	Awards Chair	Eric Rogers
	Finance Committee Chair	Ryan Sargent
	JW Books Liaison	Susan Staker
	Membership Chair	Sally Cook Roth
	MHA Liaison	Matt Harris
	Podcast Chair	Jason Smith
	Social Media Chair	Magen Edvalson
Conference & Scholarship Committee		
	Chair	Mark Staker
	Co-Chair	Rachel Killebrew
	Members	Scott Esplin
		Brian Hales
		Makoto Hunter
		Melvin Johnson
		Deb Luce
		Drew MacEachern
		Katherine Pollock
		Nancy Ross
Finance Committee		
	Chair	Ryan Sargent
	Members	William Morain
		Dan Whittemore
Awards Committee		
	Chair	Eric Rogers
	Members	
	Book Awards	John Dinger
		Makoto Hunter
		Dima Hurlbut

	Article Awards	Bryce Blankenagel Julianne Briscoe Robyn Spears David Wilson
JWHA Journal		
	Editor Associate Editor/Copy Editor Book Review Editor Production Editor Editorial Board RS Editor RS Editorial Board	Vickie Cleverly Speek Erin Metcalfe Newell Bringhurst John Hamer Craig Foster Matt Harris Katherine Hill David Howlett Melvin Johnson Rachel Killebrew Michael Marquardt Brent Metcalfe Russell Osmond William Russell Mark Scherer William Shepard Steven L. Shields Ryan Tittle Chrystal Vanel Clare Vlahos Katherine Hill Nancy Ross Steve Shields Randallynn Smith
John Whitmer Books		
	Manager Editorial Board	Seth Bryant Gary Bergera Meredith Carr Scott Esplin Peter Judd Mike Riggs Jason Smith
JWHA Newsletter		
	Editor	Reed Russell
Technical Services		
	Webmaster	Terry Erisman

Richard P. Howard Lecture

Making Peace with the Past: Community of Christ's Response to New Mormon History

The John Whitmer Historical Association is pleased to welcome Lachlan E. Mackay as our Howard Lecture for this year's conference. He currently serves as a member of the Council of Twelve Apostles for Community of Christ where he has numerous responsibilities including serving as Historic Sites director and Church History and Sacred Story Ministries Team lead. He has been a longtime member of the John Whitmer Historical Association and has served as our president. Lach earned a BA degree from the University of Missouri–Columbia in economics and Russian area studies. He briefly taught the roots of Community of Christ history in Kiev, Ukraine, and in French Polynesia. He is currently teaching in the Philippines. Lach has published numerous articles in a variety of journals and anthologies, including in the *John Whitmer Historical Association Journal* for which our organization awarded him for the best article of 1999. Married to another pastpresident of our organization, Christin Mackay, Lach has dedicated much of his life to studying and sharing the history of the Restoration. He has served as site director of the Kirtland Temple Historic Center and as director of the Joseph Smith Historic Site in Nauvoo, a position Christin later also filled.

Plenary Session

The Truth Shall Make You Free

We are honored this year to host Marlin K. Jensen as our plenary session speaker. In April 2005 he was appointed to serve as the Church Historian and Recorder for The Church of Jesus Christ of Latter-day Saints. In that role, he promoted a focused effort toward recovering and sharing the history of the tragic massacre at Mountain Meadows, Utah, in 1857. He also fostered the publication of the papers of Joseph Smith, and led in additional significant efforts at preserving the past. Marlin also served as a member of the First Quorum of the Seventy of The Church of Jesus Christ of Latter-day Saints from 1989 until 2012. During that time, he served as Executive Director of the Church Historical Department from 1996 to 1998, as Executive Director of the Family and Church History Department from 2004 until 2008, and as Executive Director of the Church History Department from 2008 until 2012. Marlin is married to Kathleen B. Jensen and together they have raised eight children and have thirty-four grandchildren and four great grandchildren. They have also raised numberless cattle at Jensen's Middle Fork Ranch in Huntsville, Utah.

Presidential Banquet & Address

Rupture and Reconciliation: Smith Family Interactions with Mountain Saints in the Midwest, 1846–1900

Kyle R. Walker

In a matter of just four years, from 1840–44, the family of the Joseph Sr. and Lucy Mack Smith was reduced by half, culminating in the deaths of Joseph, Hyrum and Samuel during that fateful summer of 1844. Those losses had a marked impact on surviving Smith family members and ushered in a new era for the family, now outnumbered by the surviving female members of the family. This presentation will explore the psychological implications of those losses on the family, surviving family member's attitude toward succession, and their decision to remain in the Midwest. It will then highlight interactions that occurred in the Midwest between the Smith family and their relatives and Saints who had gone west during the second half of the nineteenth century. Finally, it will explore the implications of those interactions and the Smith family's affiliation with the RLDS church, and the persisting challenges of being a Smith in Illinois.

Awards

In 2024, the John Whitmer Historical Association will present the following awards for books and articles published in 2023:

Smith-Pettit Best Book ($1,000)
Whittemore Best Documentary History ($500)
Alma Blair Best Biography ($500)
Pollock Best Historical Article ($500)
Suzanne Geisner & Jerry Mogg Best Theological Article ($500)
Greg Kofford Best Historical Article ($500)

We are honored to thank our sponsors, whose generous support makes this recognition possible. We are deeply grateful to George D. Smith and Martha Bradley-Evans at the Smith-Pettit Foundation, Dan and Beth Whittemore, Eric and Stephanie Rogers, Katherine Pollock, Joe Geisner and Jerry Mogg, and Greg and Cynthia Kofford.

We are deeply indebted to the dedicated members of the book and article awards committees for their meticulous evaluation of the numerous outstanding submissions. Their expertise and commitment to the field are not just invaluable but integral to the success of these awards.

We recognize the significant scholarship represented by this year's nominated books and articles. These publications represent decades of training, study, and labor that deeply enrich our community. Thank you to the nominees who contributed to the historical and theological dialogue that we find so fascinating and important. We are pleased to present the nominees for these prestigious awards.

Book Nominees

Bushman, Richard L. *Joseph Smith's Gold Plates: A Cultural History*. New York: Oxford University Press, 2023.

Feller, Gavin. *Eternity in the Ether: A Mormon Media History (The History of Media and Communication)*. Urbana: University of Illinois Press, 2023.

Handley, George B. *Lowell L. Bennion: A Mormon Educator (Introductions to Mormon Thought)*. Urbana: University of Illinois Press, 2023.

Katene, Selwyn and A. Keith Thompson. *Build for Eternity: A History of The Church of Jesus Christ of Latter-day Saints in New Zealand*. Wellington: Huia Publishers, 2023.

O'Brien, Hazel. *Irish Mormons: Reconciling Identity in Global Mormonism*. Urbana: University of Illinois Press, 2023.

Petry, Taylor G., Cory Crawford, and Eric A Eliason. *The Bible and the Latter-Day Saint Tradition*. Salt Lake City: University of Utah Press, 2023.

Saunders, Richard L. *Dale L. Morgan: Mormon and Western Histories in Transition*. Salt Lake City: University of Utah Press, 2023.

Smith, Alex D., Adam H. Petty, Jessica Nelson, and Spencer W. McBride, eds. *The Joseph Smith Papers, Documents, Volume 14: 1 January–15 May 1844*. Salt Lake City: Church Historian's Press, 2023.

Tanner Thiriot, Amy. *Slavery in Zion: A Documentary and Genealogical History of Black Lives and Black Servitude in Utah Territory, 1847-1862*. Salt Lake City: University of Utah Press, 2023.

Taysom, Stephen C. *Like a Fiery Meteor: The Life of Joseph F. Smith*. Salt Lake City: University of Utah Press, 2023.

Turley, Richard E. and Barbara Jones Brown. *Vengeance Is Mine: The Mountain Meadows Massacre and Its Aftermath*. New York: Oxford University Press, 2023.

Worthen, Bruce W. *Mormon Envoy: The Diplomatic Legacy of Dr. John Milton Bernhisel*. Urbana: University of Illinois Press, 2023.

Article Nominees

Addams, R. Jean. "The Temple Lot at Independence, Jackson County, Missouri." *John Whitmer Historical Association Journal* 43, no. 1 (2023): 55–77.

Beshears, Kyle R. "Eunice Ross Kinney: Follower of Two Mormon Prophets, Fierce Defender of Polygamy." *Journal of Mormon History* 49, no. 4 (2023): 82–123.

Eaton, Wendy. "Emmeline, Bertha, and Ada: 'Be of good comfort. Yours in Bonds, Joseph Smith.'" *John Whitmer Historical Association Journal* 43, no. 1 (2023): 164–184.

Grua, David W. and Jonathan A. Stapley. "The Letter and the Spirit: The Lord's Supper and Set Forms in Two Restoration Churches." *John Whitmer Historical Association Journal* 43, no. 1 (2023): 218–31.

Hamer, John. "The Past, Present, and Future of the Prophetic Monarchy in the Latter Day Saint Tradition." *John Whitmer Historical Association Journal* 43, no. 2 (2023): 3–28.

Harris, Matthew L. "A Tale of Two Religions: RLDS and LDS Responses to the Civil Rights Movement." *John Whitmer Historical Association Journal* 43, no. 1 (2023): 114–32.

Howlett, David J. and Nancy Ross. "Creating a Feminist Religious Counterpublic: RLDS Feminists and Women's Ordination Advocacy in America, 1970–1985." *Religion and American Culture* 33, no. 2 (2023): 220–47.

Hurlbut, David D. "A Supervisory Type of Thing: The Establishment and Impact of the Latter-day Saint Mission in Postcolonial Southeastern Nigeria." *Journal for the Institute of African Studies* 65, no. 4 (2023): 107–121.

Hurlbut, David D. "Social Projects and the RLDS Church's Mission Southeastern Nigeria, 1966–1977." *John Whitmer Historical Association Journal* 43, no. 2 (2023): 87–110.

Johnson, Janiece, and Quincy D. Newell. "'Not Only to the Gentiles, but Also to the African': Samuel Chambers and Scripture." *Church History* 92, no. 2 (2023): 357–81.

Judd, Peter. "Reorganized Latter Day Saints in London, England: A Sixty-Year Overview, 1866 to 1926." *John Whitmer Historical Association Journal* 43, no. 2 (2023): 29–43.

Mackay, Christin. "Mr. Smith Goes to Salt Lake City: Fred M. in Utah 1904–1906." *John Whitmer Historical Association Journal* 43, no. 1 (2023): 5–19.

Oman, Nathan B. "'The Blessing That's Anticipated Here Will Be Realized in the Next Life': The Development of Modern Latter-day Saint Marital Sealing Rules." *Journal of Mormon History* 49, no. 3 (2023): 103–140.

Padro, Manuel. "Cunning Distortions: Folk Christianity and Witchcraft Allegations in Early Mormon History." *Journal of Mormon History* 49, no. 1 (2023): 1–42.

Perez, William G. "Reclaiming the 'Primary Question': A New Beginning for Joseph Smith's First Vision." *BYU Studies* 62, no. 1 (2023): 149–166.

Sainsbury, Derek R. "'We Have Not Been Allowed the Liberty... to Worship As We Please' Nancy Naomi Tracy and the Denial of Latter-day Saint Religious Liberty." *Latter-day Saints and Religious Liberty: Historical and Global Perspectives*, edited by John C. Thomas and Robert T. Smith, Provo: BYU Religious Studies Center, 2023, 129–164.

Walker, Kyle R. "Another Smith Murdered Near Carthage: The Katharine Salisbury Family and the Persistence of Anti-Mormonism and Political Division in Hancock County, Illinois," *John Whitmer Historical Association Journal* 43, no. 1 (2023): 185–204.

Weber, Samuel R. "The Law of the Gospel: Shifting Interpretations of a Temple Covenant throughout Latter-day Saint History." *Journal of Mormon History* 49, no. 2 (2023): 80–97.

Scholarship Awards

We are pleased to announce our 2024 scholarship recipients: Zachary Brady, Allegra Goldstraß, Makoto Hunter, and Cyrus Simper. The recipients will be helping out around the conference, as well as presenting papers in session 221 on Friday at 11:45 a.m. and session 302 on Saturday at 8:00 a.m. Please help them feel at home at our conference.

Zachary Brady is a Utah State University senior earning his BS in English with a minor in Chemistry. He has spent several years as a student research volunteer for the Gender, Sexual, & Religious Identities Lab, (Dr. Tyler Lefevor), and is currently researching Latter-day Women's experience under the mentorship of Patrick Q. Mason for his honors capstone project. He loves creative writing and has published written works through USU's *Sink Hollow Magazine* and *Cherish: The Love of Our Mother in Heaven volume 2*. After graduation, Zach will apply to medical school, with hopes to further understand humanity through fertility medicine.

Allegra Goldstraß holds a BA in Archaeology and Religious Studies. She is currently pursuing an MA in Religious Studies at the Center of Religious Studies at Ruhr University Bochum, Germany. Her studies focus on the anthropology of religion, eschatology, and the Latter Day Saint movement. Allegra works as a research assistant on the Middle Persian Corpus Dictionary Project, where she has developed an appreciation for the methods of the digital humanities. Outside of her research, she serves as speaker of the student council, where she is involved in a variety of activities, such as the organization of events.

Cyrus Simper holds degrees from Brigham Young University–Idaho where he studied sociology and data science. He has experience as an archivist for the Guy H. Musser Archives. He currently leads projects on the early financing of the United Effort Plan and a penitentiary poetry project. His research interests include textile preservation, computer-aided indexing, machine learning, and natural language processing. Notable publications include studies on COVID-19 mental health impacts and Mormon sacred clothing. He will present his research on patriarchal blessings at the SSSR and plans to pursue a PhD in computational social science.

Makoto Hunter is a graduate student in history at the University of California, Santa Barbara. She researches the overlap of antipolygamy and antiprostitution in policy and culture as well as the shape of historical memory in the twentieth-century Latter Day Saint movement.

Thank you to those who contributed to Giving Tuesday to support scholarship. We appreciate your contributions.

Emergency Evacuation Procedures

1. Immediate Action

- Stay Calm: Stay calm and encourage others to remain calm as well.
- Listen for Instructions: Follow instructions given by event staff or over the public address system.

2. Identify Evacuation Routes

- Know the Exits: Familiarize yourself with the nearest exits and alternative routes.
- Follow Exit Signs: Look for illuminated exit signs to guide you to the nearest safe exit.

3. Evacuation Procedure

- Leave Belongings: Leave all personal belongings behind to expedite the evacuation process.
- Assist Others: Help those with disabilities or others in need of assistance if it is safe to do so.
- Do Not Use Elevators: Always use stairways instead of elevators during an evacuation.

4. Proceed to the North Lobby

- Move Quickly: Walk quickly but do not run to the designated assembly points.
- Designated Areas: Proceed to the designated assembly area.

Conference Center Floor Plan

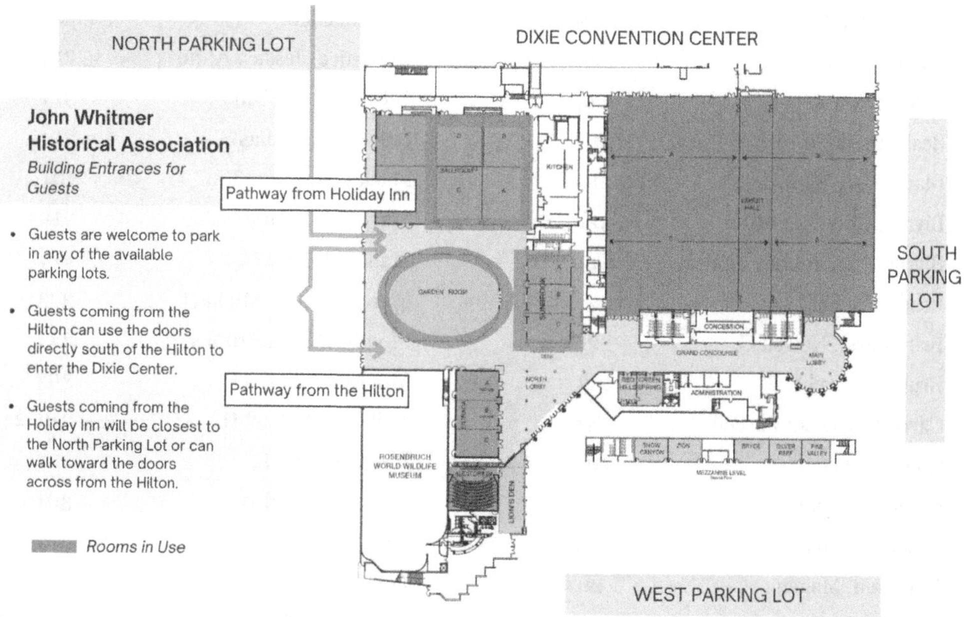

Presenters & Sessions

Addams, R. Jean	311
Alford, Kenneth L.	224
Andreason, Bryon	243
Barrus, Clair	323
Bell, Teresa Reber	244
Beshears, Kyle	213
Blais, Carly Blewster	211
Blythe, Christine Elyse	321
Blythe, Christopher James	213, 321
Brady, Zachary	221
Bringhurst, Newell G.	324l
Bruno, Cheryl L.	213
Carruth, LaJean Purcell	244
Combs, Ryan	241
Compton, Todd	324
Dinger, John S.	213
Edvalson, Magen	321
Farnes, Sherilyn	311
Gardner, Barbara Morgan	322
Gavin, Sherrie	312
Goldstraß, Allegra	302
Goodmansen, Mark	304
Hales, Brian C.	223
Hamer, John C.	313
Harris, Matthew	314, 324
Howlett, David J.	242, 314
Hunter, Makoto	221
Jensen, Marlin K.	201
Jensen, Robin Scott	214
Johnson, Melvin C.	322
Johnstun, Joseph	243
Johnstun, Shalisse Lewis	212
Killebrew, Rachel	213
Larson, Glen	241
Lawrence, Jessica Anne	214
LeCheminant, Mike	313
Literski, Nicholas S.	301
Mackay, Lachlan E.	101
Magoffin, Sean	211
Mahas, Jeffrey D.	214
Marquardt, H. Michael	323
Moody, Sharla Brooks	244
Moore, William D.	303
Neilsen, Michael H.	212, 242
Neilson, Reid L.	222
Padro, Manuel W.	301
Park, Benjamin E.	314
Plewe, Brandon	222, 241
Pollock, Katherine	303, 321
Rees, Marian Peck	312
Ross, Nancy	242, 314
Russell, William	242
Simper, Cyrus	302
Smith, Alex D.	214
Smith, Jason R.	224
Taylor, David R.	304
Walden, Barbara	321
Walker, Kyle R.	331
Watson, Kirk	223

Thank you, presenters and session chairs, you make the conference a success!

Agenda at a Glance

Thursday, September 12, 2024

Mountain Time Location	Session Presenter	Agenda Item
4:00 - 6:00 p.m. **Outside Ballroom**		Registration Open
6:00 - 6:30 p.m. **Ballroom C & D**	Kyle R. Walker, presiding	Annual Business Meeting
	Sharla Brooks Moody	Welcome to St. George
7:00 - 8:00 p.m. **Ballroom C & D**	**Keynote** **101** Lachlan E. Mackay	*Richard P. Howard Lecture* Making Peace with the Past: Community of Christ's Response to New Mormon History
8:00 - 10:00 p.m. **Garden Room**		Reception
	Alex Baugh	Magic in the Desert
9:00 p.m. **Garden Room**		1st Time Attendees Meet & Greet

Friday, September 13, 2024

Mountain Time Location	Session Presenter	Agenda Item
8:30 - 10:00 a.m. **Garden Room**		Breakfast (included in registration)
8:30 - 9:30 a.m. **Ballroom C & D** Chair: Reid L. Neilson	**Plenary** **201** Marlin K. Jensen	The Truth Shall Make You Free
9:30 - 10:00 a.m. **Ballroom A & B**		Break ❋Exhibits Open❋ ❋Silent Auction❋ ❋Visit JW Books❋
10:00 - 11:15 a.m. **Sunbrook A** Chair: Casey Paul Griffiths	**211** Sean Magoffin	Birth Control: A Case Study of the Relationship between Doctrine, Policy, and a Changing World
	Carly Blewster Blais	Evolving Practice and Policy in Latter-day Saint Missionary Work
10:00 - 11:15 a.m. **Sunbrook B** Chair: Matthew Harris	**212** Michael H. Nielsen	The Arrival and Activities of Reorganized Latter Day Saints in Southwest Utah
	Shalisse Lewis Johnstun	If the Past is a Foreign Country, Who's Teaching Kids the Language?
10:00 - 11:15 a.m. **Sunbrook C** Chair: Nancy Ross	**213** Cheryl L. Bruno Christopher James Blythe Kyle Beshears John S. Dinger Rachel Killebrew	Come Up Hither to Zion: William Marks and the Mormon Concept of Gathering
10:00 - 11:15 a.m. **Ballroom C & D** Chair: Matthew C. Godfrey	**Panel 214** Alex D. Smith Jessica Anne Lawrence Jeffrey D. Mahas Robin Scott Jensen	The Life and Faith of William Clayton: Insights from His Nauvoo Journal
11:15 - 11:45 a.m. **Ballroom A & B**		Break ❋Exhibits Open❋ ❋Silent Auction❋ ❋Visit JW Books❋

Sunbrook A Chair: Sherry Mesle-Morain	Zachary Brady	Saint Women's Power and Authority
	Makoto Hunter	World Religions and Historical Imagination in Exploring the Book of Mormon: Teaching Scriptural Pasts and Presents to Twentieth-century Reorganized Youth
11:45 a.m. - 1:00 p.m. **Sunbrook B** Chair: Gary Boatright	**222** Brandon Plewe	This Branch of the Church: the Evolution of Local Church Administration
	Reid L. Neilson	From Parowan to the Pacific: The overland travel of China missionaries from Southern Utah to Southern California in 1852
11:45 a.m. - 1:00 p.m. **Sunbrook C** Chair: Deb Luce	**223** Brian C. Hales	Using Artificial Intelligence to Predict the Skills Needed to Reproduce the Book of Mormon
	Kirk Watson	A "Newsie Messiah": the Lives and Teachings of Israel A. J. Dennis
11:45 a.m. - 1:00 p.m. **Ballroom C & D** Chair: Ryan Robinson	**224** Kenneth L. Alford	Hyrum Smith and Nauvoo Freemasonry
	Jason R. Smith	Telling the Truth: A Journey in Documentary History of the Church of Christ (Temple Lot)
1:00 - 1:15 p.m. **Ballroom A & B**		Break ❋Exhibits Open❋ ❋Silent Auction❋ ❋Visit JW Books❋
1:15 - 2:15 p.m. **Garden Room**	**Awards Ceremony** Eric Paul Rogers	Awards Ceremony & Banquet - included in registration fee
2:15 - 2:45 p.m. **Ballroom A & B**		Break ❋Exhibits Open❋ ❋Silent Auction❋ ❋Visit JW Books❋
2:45- 4:00 p.m. **Sunbrook A** Chair: R. Jean Addams	**241** Ryan Combs Brandon Plewe	Hamblin missions from St. George to Hopi Villages
	Glen Larson	Creating Micro Economic Peace Settlement with the United Orders (1873–1877): Knab, Orderville, and St. George Settlements
2:45- 4:00 p.m. **Sunbrook B** Chair: Myra Elliott	**242** William Russell read by Michael H. Nielsen	Both RLDS and LDS Churches Erred in Their Method of Presidential Succession
	Nancy Ross David J.Howlett	Beehive Girls and the Priesthood: Reactions to Women's Ordination and Feminism in LDS Church Curriculum in the 1970s and 1980s
2:45- 4:00 p.m. **Sunbrook C** Chair: Eric Paul Rogers	**243** Joseph Johnstun	Armed Men, Furious Men, With Murder In Their Hearts: The Men Who Killed Joseph and Hyrum Smith—Claims, Accusations, and Pus-filled Wounds
	Bryon Andreasen	Did Joseph Smith Really Faint?—The June 25, 1844 Militia Review in Carthage, Illinois
2:45- 4:00 p.m. **Ballroom C & D** Chair: Melvin Clarno Johnson	**244** LaJean Purcell Carruth	Striving to Make Peace with the Mountain Meadows Massacre
	Teresa Reber Bell Sharla Brooks Moody	The Influence of Juanita Brooks on Restoration History
5:00 - 7:00 p.m. Downtown St. George Juanita Brooks Property		Walking Tours - Preregistration Required

Saturday, September 14, 2024

Mountain Time Location	Session Presenter	Agenda Item
7:30 - 9:00 a.m. **Garden Room**		Breakfast - included in registration fee.
8:00 - 9:15 a.m. **Sunbrook A** Chair: Rachel Killebrew	**301** Manuel W. Padro	Playing with the Enlightenment's Shadows: 19th-Century Witchcraft Hysteria in Early Mormon History
	Nicholas S. Literski	Keep This from Vulgar Eyes: Mormonism's Tradition of Hidden Books
8:00 - 9:15 a.m. **Sunbrook B** Chair: Kyle R. Walker	**302** Allegra Goldstraß	Restoration Eschatologies and their Conceptual Metaphors
	Cyrus Simper	John Tanner Clark and the Enigma of the "One Mighty and Strong"
8:00 - 9:15 a.m. **Sunbrook C** Chair: Jason R. Smith	**303** William D. Moore	RLDS Reunion Grounds: Change and Continuity
	Katherine Pollock	RLDS Young Adults on Mission: Older Youth Service Corps, 1964-1973
8:00 - 9:15 a.m. **Ballroom C & D** Chair: Bradley Armstrong	**304** Mark Goodmansen	Prelude to the Oregon and Mormon Trails: From the Secret of South Pass in 1813 to the Ultimatum Map of 1838
	David R. Taylor	Scandal, Suicide, and Strife in a Small Southern Utah Community
9:15 - 9:45 a.m. **Ballroom A & B**		Break ❋Exhibits Open❋ ❋Silent Auction❋ ❋Visit JW Books❋
9:45 - 10:30 a.m. **Sunbrook A** Chair: Susan Staker	**311** R. Jean Addams	John Beck's Fabulous Mine: An Outpost in the Tintic Mountains of Early Utah Territory
	Sherilyn Farnes	Some Friends and Also Brethren: Religious "Outposts" in the Western Missouri Borderlands, 1825–1835
9:45 - 10:30 a.m. **Sunbrook B** Chair: Magen Edvalson	**312** Sherrie Gavin	Early Mormon Women and the Word of Wisdom
	Marian Peck Rees	Sarah Maria Mousley Cannon: Making Peace with "the days of your poverty"
9:45 - 10:30 a.m. **Sunbrook C** Chair: William Morain	**313** John C. Hamer	Reconciliation with First Nations Peoples/Native Americans on the Eve of the Book of Mormon's Bicentennial
	Mike LeCheminant	Striving to Make Peace with the Mountain Meadows Massacre
9:45 - 10:30 a.m. **Ballroom C & D** Chair: Newell Bringhurst	**314** Benjamin E. Park David J. Howlett Nancy Ross Matthew Harris	New American Zion: Benjamin E Park's American Zion a New History of Mormonism
10:30 - 11:00 a.m. **Ballroom A & B**		Break ❋Exhibits Open❋ ❋Silent Auction❋ ❋Visit JW Books❋
11:00 a.m. - 12:15 p.m. **Ballroom C & D** Chair: Sally Roth	**Panel 321** Barbara Walden Christine Elyse Blythe Christopher James Blythe Katherine Pollock Magen Edvalson	Summers Well Spent: Reminiscing on Alma Blair and the Internship Program at Nauvoo and Kirtland

11:00 a.m. - 12:15 p.m. **Sunbrook A** Chair: Sherrie Gavin	**322** Barbara Morgan Gardner	Rebecca Wheeler Wright
	Melvin C. Johnson	The Women of the "Texas Epidemic" Come to Pine Valley
11:00 a.m. - 12:15 p.m. **Sunbrook B** Chair: Christin Mackay	**323** Clair Barrus	The Revelations of Heber C. Kimball
	H. Michael Marquardt	The End Times According to Latter Day Saint Joseph Smith Senior
11:00 a.m. - 12:15 p.m. **Sunbrook C** Chair: Mike Allen	**324** Todd Compton	Joseph Hyrum Grant, Heber J. Grant, and the Passing of LDS Plural Marriage
	Newell Bringhurst	Heber Bennion: Heber J. Grant's Rogue Brother-in Law
	Matthew Harris	Hugh B. Brown confronts Polygamy within his own Family
12:30 - 5:30 p.m.		Bus Tours - Advance registration required
6:30 - 8:30 p.m. **Garden Room**	**331** Kyle R. Walker	*Presidential Banquet & Address* - Advance registration required The First Family of the Restoration
		2024–2025 Board Installation
Mountain Time Location	**Session Presenter**	**Agenda Item**
Sunday, September 24, 2023		
9:00- 10:00 a.m. St. George Tabernacle	**Hymn Fest** Brian C. Hales	Singing the Songs of Restoration

Welcome First Time JWHA Attendees !

You are invited to attend a meet and greet in the Garden Room

Thursday, September 12, 2024

Following the Richard P. Howard Lecture

- Meet keynote speaker Lachlan Mackay
- Visit with fellow attendees
- Opportunity to win a drawing for a **$50** Visa gift card

Learn more about JWHA

JWHA 2024 Annual Conference

Abstracts and Biographical Sketches

Keynote 101 Richard P. Howard Lecture (7:00 p.m., Thursday, September 12)

Title: Making Peace with the Past: Community of Christ's Response to New Mormon History by Lachlan E. Mackay

Abstract: Community of Christ members and leaders have had a complicated history with their history, sometimes embracing it, sometimes denying it, and sometimes doing both at the same time. The arrival of New Mormon History in the second half of the twentieth century challenged many foundational myths, making the relationship even more complex. It has been a long, slow, and at times painful process, but the first decades of the twenty-first century have seen significant progress made as the church makes peace with its past.

Biographical Sketch: Lachlan E. Mackay is a past president of the John Whitmer Historical Association and now serves in Community of Christ's Council of Twelve Apostles where he oversees the Northeast USA Mission Field. Additional assignments include serving as the Director of Historic Sites and lead for the Church History and Sacred Story Team.

A native of Independence, Missouri, Lach received a Bachelor of Arts in Economics and Russian Area Studies from the University of Missouri-Columbia. His past publications have focused on Kirtland Temple, the Smith family properties in Nauvoo, and the visual image of Joseph Smith, including most recently extensive work on the Smith Larsen daguerreotype.

Plenary 201 (8:30 a.m., Friday, September 13)

Title: The Truth Shall Make You Free by Marlin K. Jensen

Abstract: The Mountain Meadows is a highland desert valley in Southern Utah where approximately 120 men, women, and children, mainly Arkansas emigrants bound for California, were massacred in September 1857. The full story of this tragedy, including the culpability and motives of the principal perpetrators, local leaders and members of The Church of Jesus Christ of Latter-day Saints, was slow to emerge. The result was historical confusion and ill feeling between church members and descendants of the victims that persisted for nearly 150 years.

In the early 2000's senior leaders of the LDS church authorized and gave full editorial control to professional historians in its history department to comprehensively study the massacre and to write a book fully detailing their findings. The resulting book, *Massacre at Mountain Meadows,* is an unflinching account of the tragic event that concludes that the perpetrators of the massacre were indeed members of The Church of Jesus Christ of Latter-day Saints, aided by Indians. The emergence and admission of the truth about the massacre by the LDS church and a cooperatively staged sesquicentennial commemoration of the massacre in 2007 were catalysts in changing minds and hearts on all sides of this contentious issue.

Recent years have seen a remarkable reconciliation occur between the church and descendants of the victims. Lasting friendships have been formed, memorial gatherings have been held, cooperative efforts have been made to preserve and protect the massacre site as a hallowed burial ground, and vital lessons of the past and present are being preserved and shared in an atmosphere of mutual trust and understanding.

Biographical Sketch: Marlin K. Jensen served as a member of the First Quorum of the Seventy of The Church of Jesus Christ of Latter-day Saints from 1989 until 2012. During that time, he served as Executive Director of the Church Historical Department from 1996 to 1998, as Executive Director of the Family and Church History Department from 2004 until 2008, and as Executive Director of the Church History Department from 2008 until 2012. In April 2005, he also became the first Church Historian and Recorder to serve since 1997. In these roles, he oversaw efforts to research and share the truth about tragic events surrounding the Mountain Meadows Massacre. He was given emeritus status in October 2012. Since then, he has returned to his real passion of ranching as a partner in Jensen's Middle Fork Ranch

Session 211: (10:00 a.m., Friday September 13)

Title: Birth Control: A Case Study of the Relationship between Doctrine, Policy, and a Changing World by Sean Magoffin

Abstract: An oft confused difference among members of The Church of Jesus Christ of Latter-Day Saints is that between policy and doctrine. In an ever-shifting society church policies seem to be changing constantly while doctrine remains unchanged. Birth control is a wonderful case study for understanding the relationship between doctrine and policy along with the influences that attribute to policy changes. The church's first policies and teachings about birth control likely had many influences from doctrinal understanding, societal movements, and past church practices such as polygamy. Birth control in the US was illegal for many years which aligned with church teachings. However, as Margaret Sanger and her birth control movement gained popularity and acceptance things began to change. Along with major changes in the world and American society, the church changed their policy on birth control. The ability to understand the difference between doctrine and policy is critical to keeping our testimony of the Savior firm despite the changes in the church that inevitably will come and help us have the right lens to understand the church's evolving views toward birth control.

Biographical Sketch: Sean Magoffin is a junior at Brigham Young University studying mechanical engineering. Sean is a lifelong member of The Church of Jesus Christ of Latter-Day Saints and graduated from their seminary program. He served a mission in Everett, Washington using American Sign Language while working with the deaf community. Despite his major being mechanical engineering, he spends much of his free time studying the history and teachings of The Church of Jesus Christ of Latter-Day Saints and is especially interested in providing faithful explanations of some more controversial and difficult topics.

Title: Evolving Practice and Policy in Latter-day Saint Missionary Work by Carly Blewster Blais

Abstract: The Church of Jesus Christ of Latter-day Saints has expanded its way of teaching and proselytizing since the first missionary's call in 1830. In this presentation, we will address the positives and negatives of these changes, and how the evolving full-time missionary program has affected converts, members, and the missionaries themselves. This has been done through the transformation of rule handbooks and teaching manuals, alongside many suggestions and statements from church leaders. We have analyzed mission practices throughout the church's existence, and we will propose some alterations to the modern-day missionary program in order to benefit all involved in the work. In order to create the best experience within the missionary field, we believe that by knowing its history and by offering recommendations, this goal can be accomplished. We also believe certain changes to missionary policies may allow for improved physical and mental health for male and female missionaries.

Biographical Sketch: Carly Blewster Blais, a twenty-two-year-old student attending Brigham Young University, is from Phoenix, Arizona. During her upbringing, Carly cultivated a passion for dancing and performing. While at BYU, she is studying exercise and wellness with hopes to become a medical doctor. Alongside her studies, Carly is actively involved in cancer research, having dedicated over a year and a half to a biochemistry research lab, reflecting her deep passion for medicine and healing. She has developed a special interest in church history that began while serving her full-time mission for The Church of Jesus Christ of Latter-day Saints in Albuquerque, New Mexico. Her commitment to understanding church history is intertwined with her mission to serve and uplift others, displaying her broader dedication to community and the collective welfare.

Session 212 (10:00 a.m., Friday, September 13)

Title: The Arrival and Activities of Reorganized Latter Day Saints in Southwest Utah by Michael H. Nielsen

Abstract: It is well known in RLDS history that Edmund Briggs and Alexander McCord were the first commissioned evangelists of the Reorganized church to arrive in Utah in 1863 in a long-term endeavor to turn the Mormons from perceived tyrannical leaders and devilish doctrines. What remains largely untold, and is the aim of my paper, is the story and impact of RLDS missionaries and members in pioneer southwest Utah. Early RLDS missionaries inconsistently but resolutely trod into places like Saint George and Beaver making known their message and seeking to find the disaffected and questioning. Though in no way comprehensive, the paper substantially highlights the labors of these under-appreciated and lesser-known individuals from the 1860s to the 1910s. It also elevates our collective understanding of peripheral dissent in rural pioneer Utah. After fifty years of this endeavor, the costs in human labor and financial resources simply outweighed any real profit in new believers and publicity.

Biographical Sketch: Michael H. Nielsen is a native of Saint George, Utah, and alumnus of Dixie State (Utah Tech) University where he won the history student of the year award for which he got a fancy rock despite not learning about that fact until later. He worked as an intern at the Joseph Smith Historic Site in Nauvoo, Illinois; the Kirtland Temple Historic Site in Kirtland, Ohio; and as a docent at Silver Reef Museum in Leeds, Utah. When he is not researching or reading, he enjoys hiking, amateurly attempting to play the piano, and homemade chocolate chip cookies.

Title: If the Past is a Foreign Country, Who's Teaching Kids the Language? by Shalisse Lewis Johnstun

Abstract: L. P. Hartley's 1953 declaration that "The past is a foreign country" has been widely accepted, and some historians have taken it as a mantra. Many young students have not been given the chance to experience history in an engaging way. This new generation of students wants to know why they should study history at all when a quick Google search will give you the who, what, and where? The problem for current historians is how do we engage the next generation, teach them to use the different lenses of a historian to discover the *why*. Shalisse looks at how historians can partner with teachers and open up as a community to find ways to help the next generation find their way to this beautiful, complex country we call history.

Biographical Sketch: Shalisse Lewis Johnstun is a kick-ass high school educator/adjunct professor/raptor-wrangler on a mission to ignite a love of lifelong learning in her students. Many students will tell you that history is boring or has nothing to do with them. It seems that it is only as we grow older that we appreciate the value of studying the past. Shalisse teaches that there is a difference between knowledge and information. Information—the *what*—can be accessed and recalled quickly, particularly in the digital age. Knowledge requires analysis of the *why* and the *how*.

Session 213 (10:00 a.m., Friday, September 13)

Title: Come Up Hither to Zion: William Marks and the Mormon Concept of Gathering by Cheryl L. Bruno, Christopher James Blythe, Kyle Beshears, John S. Dinger, Rachel Killebrew

Abstract: Three reviewers with different areas of expertise: LDS, Community of Christ, and the James Strang movement, comment on a new biography, "Come Up Hither to Zion: William Marks and the Mormon Concept of Gathering," by Cheryl L. Bruno and John S. Dinger. William Marks is the most important early Mormon figure that you may know next to nothing about!

Biographical Sketch: Cheryl L. Bruno has a BS in recreation management from Greensboro College, Greensboro, NC, and did graduate work in educational psychology at Brigham Young University, Provo, UT. She is an independent researcher in Mormon studies, with an interest in the intersection of Mormonism and Freemasonry, Mormon esotericism and Mormon plural marriage. Cheryl is the author of *Method Infinite: Freemasonry and the Mormon Restoration* with Joe Steve Swick III and Nicholas S. Literski. She is editor of *Secret Covenants: New Insights on Mormon Polygamy*. Her publications can be found in the *Journal of Religion and Society*, the *John Whitmer Historical Association Journal*, and the *Journal of Mormon History*. Most recently, she and John S. Dinger have completed a biography on early Mormon leader William Marks.

Biographical Sketch: Kyle R. Beshears (PhD, Southern Baptist Theological Seminary) is a minister in Mobile, Alabama, and an independent researcher in Mormon studies. His dissertation focused on the history of the Church of Jesus Christ of Latter Day Saints (Strangite) after the death of its founder, James J. Strang. He is the author of the forthcoming *40 Questions about Mormonism* (Kregel Academic) and has taught religious studies at the University of Mobile.

Biographical Sketch: John S. Dinger is a graduate of the S. J. Quinney College of Law, University of Utah, Salt Lake City. In addition to his juris doctorate, he holds degrees in political science and history from the University of Utah. He has published in the *Journal of Mormon History*, *John Whitmer Historical Association Journal*, *Idaho Law Review*, and *Utah Law Review*. His book *The Nauvoo High Council and City Minutes* won Best Documentary Book Award from the Mormon History Association and the Best Book Award from the John Whitmer Historical Association. He is an attorney in Boise, Idaho.

Biographical Sketch: Rachel Killebrew has a BS in education and history from William Jewell College, and an MLIS from the University of Missouri. She is the World Church Librarian-Archivist and Records Manager for the Community of Christ Church. Rachel is a past president and board member of the John Whitmer Historical Association.

Biographical Sketch: Christopher James Blythe is an assistant professor of folklore and Latter-day Saint literature at Brigham Young University. He is the author of *Terrible Revolution: Latter-day Saints and the American Apocalypse* (Oxford, 2020) and co-editor of *Open Canon: Scriptures of the Latter Day Saint Tradition* (Utah, 2022). Blythe also hosts the podcast, Angels and Seerstones with his wife, Christine.

Panel 214 (10:00 a.m., Friday, September 13)

Title: The Life and Faith of William Clayton: Insights from His Nauvoo Journal by Alex D. Smith, Jessica Anne Lawrence, Jeffrey D. Mahas, Robin Scott Jensen

Abstract: William Clayton's personal journal is one of the most important contemporaneous sources for understanding the Nauvoo era of Mormon history. This session will consider some of the historical contributions that the project team has observed while preparing this anticipated manuscript for publication. Papers will examine Clayton's creation of the journal and its subsequent provenance as well as significant content themes such as church business practices and finance, Joseph Smith's activities during his final years, Nauvoo social life, and Clayton's own character traits and faith as depicted in the pages of the journal.

Biographical Sketch: Alex D. Smith Alex is a historian with the Church History Department of The Church of Jesus Christ of Latter-day Saints. He served as a volume editor of six volumes in the Journals and Documents series of the Joseph Smith Papers. He currently leads the William Clayton Nauvoo journals project and is working on a book that explores the causes of Joseph Smith's assassination.

Biographical Sketch: Jessica Anne Lawrence is an editor in the Church History Department of The Church of Jesus Christ of Latter-day Saints, working on *Saints, Carry On,* and the William Clayton Nauvoo journal projects. She received a bachelor's degree in psychology from Brigham Young University and is receiving a second bachelor's degree in English from Utah Valley University.

Biographical Sketch: Jeffrey D. Mahas received a BA from Brigham Young University and an MA in history from the University of Utah. He has worked for the Church History Department since 2013.

Biographical Sketch: Robin Scott Jensen is a historian at the Church History Library and served as editor and archivist for the Joseph Smith Papers and coedited the five volumes in the Revelations and Translations series (published 2009, 2011, 2015, 2018, and 2021). In 2005 he earned an MA degree in American history from Brigham Young University, and in 2009 he earned a second MA in library and information science with an archival concentration from the University of Wisconsin–Milwaukee. In 2019 he earned a PhD in history at the University of Utah. He is currently studying the textual culture of Mormonism and launching a Mormon book history program at the Church History Library.

Session 221 (11:45 a.m., Friday, September 12)

Title: Off The Stand, But Standing Up: A Contemporary View of Latter-day Saint Women's Power and Authority by Zachary Brady

Abstract: From women being ordered off the stand by men to maintain long-established common meeting practices, to questionable statements during the 2024 Worldwide Relief Society Devotional, recent decisions made by leadership within The Church of Jesus Christ of Latter-day Saints seemed to have kindled a frenzy, igniting outpours of outrage on social media concerning the churches inequality of priesthood power and authority between men and women. This paper explores these inequalities by examining the differences between priesthood power and governing power and attempting to unlink power and authority with traditional gender roles by looking at the history of the early Relief Society. Like our Heavenly Parents—who cocreate side by side—women in the church deserve to have their voices represented alongside their brothers in Christ.

Biographical Sketch: Zachary Brady is a Utah State University senior earning his BS in English with a minor in chemistry. He has spent several years as a student research volunteer for the Gender, Sexual, & Religious Identities Lab, (Dr. Tyler Lefevor), and is currently researching Latter-day women's experience under the mentorship of Patrick Q. Mason for his honors capstone project. He loves creative writing and has published written works through USU's *Sink Hollow Magazine* and *Cherish: The Love of Our*

Mother in Heaven volume 2. After graduation, Zach will apply to medical school, with hopes to further understand humanity through fertility medicine.

Title: World Religions and Historical Imagination in Exploring the Book of Mormon: Teaching Scriptural Pasts and Presents to Twentieth-century Reorganized Youth by Makoto Hunter

Abstract: In 1960, the Reorganized Church of Jesus Christ of Latter Day Saints (today known as Community of Christ) published *Exploring the Book of Mormon*, a reader for youth. Written by Biloine Young and illustrated by Edith Brockway, this series taught the Book of Mormon to middle school-age members of the Reorganization. This paper will explore *Exploring the Book of Mormon* by placing it in the wider Christian contexts of the World Religions paradigm and biblical visualization.

Biographical Sketch: Makoto Hunter is a graduate student in history at the University of California, Santa Barbara. She researches the overlap of antipolygamy and antiprostitution in policy and culture as well as the shape of historical memory in the twentieth century Latter Day Saint movement.

Session 222 (11:45 a.m., Friday, September 13)

Title: This Branch of the Church: the Evolution of Local Church Administration by Brandon Plewe

Abstract: During Joseph Smith's lifetime, he gradually introduced localized institutions to minister to the growing church, such as branches, bishops, stakes, and wards. Yet these operated quite differently from anything we would recognize today. After his death, the congregations of the church that followed Brigham Young continued to evolve into a wide variety of localized practices, including some that have survived to the present, and some that may seem very strange. After decades of little central effort to standardize, President Young and the Twelve completely reorganized every ward, branch, and stake in 1877 according to a common standard that is remarkably similar to the present. By building a comprehensive database of the organizational history of every early church unit, and deconstructing our assumptions (and the assumptions of past historians) about administrative patterns, we are starting to understand how and why this evolution occurred.

Biographical Sketch: Brandon Plewe has taught geography, GIS, and cartography at Brigham Young University since 1997. His research focuses on historical cartography, especially mapping the history of the Intermountain West and The Church of Jesus Christ of Latter-day Saints. He and his wife Jamie have five children and four grandchildren.

Title: From Parowan to the Pacific: The overland travel of China missionaries from Southern Utah to Southern California in 1852 by Reid L. Neilson

Abstract: In August 1852, Brigham Young called over one hundred men to leave their families and serve proselyting missions throughout the world. More specifically, he assigned four men to evangelize the Chinese in Hong Kong, then a British colony in the strategic South China Sea. These men, along with about three dozen other missionaries called to serve in the Pacific Frontier Basin, left the pioneer settlement of Parowan, Utah, then the furthest south colony of the Latter-day Saints, and crossed the Mojave Desert as the followed the "Southern Route" to San Bernardino, California, and then on to the Pacific port of Los Angeles at San Pedro. Their journey lasted several weeks and was fraught with dangers and challenges. My paper will tell their story and what it meant for the larger Latter-day Saint experience in the Asia-Pacific world.

Biographical Sketch: Dr. Reid L. Neilson joined the BYU faculty in August 2022, when he began leading as the assistant academic vice president for religious scholarly publications, a newly created position at the university. He oversees three organizations on campus: the Neal A. Maxwell Institute for Religious Scholarship, the Religious Studies Center, and BYU Studies. Prior to rejoining the faculty at BYU, Dr. Neilson and his wife, Shelly, served as the leaders of the Washington DC North Mission. Before his mission presidency, Neilson was appointed Assistant Church Historian and Recorder of the Church in 2015. He also worked as the managing director of the Church History Department from 2010 to 2019. In 2006, Dr. Neilson began his academic career as an assistant professor of church history and doctrine in Religious Education at BYU, where he received the university's Young Scholar Award. He is the author and award-winning editor of more than thirty books, including *Restless Pilgrim: Andrew Jenson's Quest for Latter-day Saint History* (with Scott D. Marianno in 2022). A native of Orange County, California, Neilson received a bachelor's degree (international relations) and two master's degrees (business management and American history) from BYU and holds a doctorate in religious studies (American religions) from the University of North Carolina at Chapel Hill. He later completed the Harvard Business School's General Management Program.

Session 223 (11:45 a.m., Friday, September 13)

Title: Using Artificial Intelligence to Predict the Skills Needed to Reproduce the Book of Mormon by Brian C. Hales

Abstract: According to available historical documents, Joseph Smith dictated the Book of Mormon to scribes without notes in less than three months. By identifying specific literary characteristics of that dictation as found in the 1830 printing, artificial intelligence (AI) chatbots can predict the skills needed to create a similar narrative. Accordingly, this question was compiled:

"What skills would be needed to compose and dictate in three months without notes a book with: 269,320 words; Sentences: 6,852; Average sentence: 39.3 words; Reading level: eighth grade; Dialect: Early Modern English; Unique words: 5,600; College-level vocabulary words: dozens; Original proper nouns: 170; Distinct titles for God: over 100; Literary style: Christological epic, lengthy, complex; Characters: 207; Socio-geographic groups: 44; Chronological systems: 3; Geographical locations in the fictional destination: 149; Geographical locations in known world: at least 15; Storylines: 77 major plus more minor; Genealogies greater than twenty generations: 2; Flashbacks and embedded storylines: 5; Ecological references: 2,065; Monetary Weights: 12; Sermons: 63 comprising over 87,000 words; Sermon topics: over 80; Parallel poetic devices like chiasmus: over 400; Bible intertextuality: at least 650 allusions; Editorial promises: at least 121; Internally fulfilled prophecies: at least 120; and Subjects discussed with precision include biblical law, olive tree husbandry, and warfare tactics?"

This presentation will review the skills identified by eleven artificial intelligence chatbots: Chat GPT 4 (subscription), Chat GPT 3 (free version), Google Bard, Anthropic' s Claude, iAsk.AI, Microsoft Copilot, Meta's Llama2-7B and Llama2-13B, Inflection's PI, Quora's POE, and Perplexity. It will also compare those predictions to the descriptions of Joseph Smith's 1829 skillset.

Biographical Sketch: Brian C. Hales {brianhales@msn.com} is the author or co-author of seven books dealing with plural marriage, including the three-volume *Joseph Smith's Polygamy: History and Theology* (Salt Lake City: Greg Kofford Books, 2013). He is a retired anesthesiologist. His new book, *Authoring the Book of Mormon* should be out next year.

Title: A "Newsie Messiah": the Lives and Teachings of Israel A. J. Dennis by Kirk Watson

Abstract: The life of "Israel" A. J. Dennis (1852–1933) has always been told in a fragmentary manner. This paper will cover his life holistically as a dissident in multiple religious traditions: from a Methodist holiness revivalist he became a preacher for the Seventh-day Adventists, and eventually came to Utah and joined the LDS church. As an End-Times prophecy enthusiast, he had visions that led him to found the "Church of the First Born", and then become the leader of the "Restored Church of the Messiah" and the Davidic King of the "Restored Kingdom of God". Throughout his life he was declared insane, he was persecuted, prosecuted, incarcerated, and even interdicted by federal authorities, all for the sake of his unique religious mission.

Biographical Sketch: Kirk Watson was born and raised in Sanpete County, Utah, where some of the events described in his presentation took place. He studied at the University of Utah and the University of Denver. He and his wife have lived in London and Belfast, where their two children were born. Since 2015, he has worked in the digital library and archive at the Marriott Library, University of Utah.

Session 224 (11:45 a.m., Friday, September 13)

Title: Hyrum Smith and Nauvoo Freemasonry by Kenneth L. Alford

Abstract: Hyrum Smith, an older brother of Joseph Smith Jr, played an important role in the organization and expansion of Freemasonry in Nauvoo, Illinois—serving as Senior Warden pro tem, Master pro tem, and Worshipful Master of the Nauvoo Masonic Lodge. This presentation will share interesting information and anecdotes regarding the role Freemasonry played in the life and history of Nauvoo and the Smith family's long association with Freemasonry—beginning with Hyrum's father, Joseph Smith Sr. Summary demographic information will also be shared about the many hundreds of Nauvoo citizens who became Freemasons based on the Nauvoo Masonic Lodge Minutes and other historical records.

Biographical Sketch: Kenneth L. Alford is a professor of Church History and Doctrine at Brigham Young University and a retired U.S. Army Colonel. Prior to teaching at BYU, he served as a professor of computer science at the U.S. Military Academy at West Point, New York and as a department chair and professor of strategic leadership and organizational behavior at the National Defense University in Washington, DC. Ken served in numerous assignments during almost thirty years on active duty in the Army. He has published and presented on a wide variety of subjects—authoring or editing a dozen books and over 150 articles.

Title: Telling the Truth: A Journey in Documentary History of the Church of Christ (Temple Lot) by Jason R. Smith

Abstract: For the past several years, I have been combing through publications and periodicals of the Church of Christ (Temple Lot), headquartered in Independence, MO in order to produce a documentary history of this small, but unique, branch of the Smith-Rigdon Movement. During this process, I have collected (mostly digitally) thousands of articles and other official documents pertaining to the church's rich history. In my presentation, I would like to take the audience through a brief tour of what I have discovered. The journey would begin with early church records and would then explore statistical patterns and trends in the church's official periodicals, as well as discussing how major and minor theological changes were expressed through the press. I would also include commentary on how these were influenced by and responded to interactions with other Restoration churches.

Biographical Sketch: Jason has a BA in history from Cameron University and is currently working toward an MA in religious studies at Chicago Theological Seminary. He works as the IT manager for a local governmental agency in Duncan, Oklahoma, where he lives with his wife and too many dogs. Jason also serves on the board of JWHA and has an avid interest in all of the many expressions of the Smith-Rigdon Movement.

Session 241 (2:45 p.m., Friday, September 13)

Title: Hamblin Missions from St. George to Hopi Villages by Ryan Combs, Brandon Plewe

Abstract: Jacob Hamblin led multiple missions from St. George to the Hopi villages in northeastern Arizona. These missions required crossing the Colorado River, the route was based on information from the Old Spanish Trail and led to Latter-day Saint settlements in northern Arizona. One of those missions in 1862/1863 was documented by John Steele. Steele was an Irish convert who was a member of the Nauvoo Legion, Mormon Battalion, first postmaster of Las Vegas, and amateur physician. One of the most fascinating parts of his records is a hand drawn map of the route taken. We will go through an analysis of the map including plotting the map to real-world locations.

Biographical Sketch: Ryan Combs has a BA in Middle East history and an MS in library science, until recently he worked for the Church History Department, he still works for The Church of Jesus Christ of Latter-day Saints but now in the IT department. He also previously worked as a religious studies librarian at the Harold B. Lee Library at BYU. He lives in Provo with his wife Elizabeth and four children.

Biographical Sketch: Brandon Plewe has taught geography, GIS, and cartography at Brigham Young University since 1997. His research focuses on historical cartography, especially mapping the history of the Intermountain West and The Church of Jesus Christ of Latter-day Saints. He and his wife Jamie have five children and four grandchildren.

Title: Creating Micro Economic Peace Settlement with the United Orders (1873-1877): Knab, Orderville, and St. George Settlements by Glen Larson

Abstract: The creation between 1873–77 of 220 Latter-day Saint communities known as United Orders helped small settlements in the Intermountain West respond to the cyclic recessions of the 1870s. At that time, economic inconsistency plagued the United States. The Orders continued to have an impact in the southwest desert communities up until the creation of the Federal Reserve System in the 1930s.

This paper examines three of these orders in Southern Utah. What Brigham Young established was different than Joseph Smith's "Law of Consecration and Stewardship." His United Orders created tension between Church leaders and members. But they also brought together the basic micro economic foundation for individual, family, and community togetherness, thus creating sustainable peace. These United Orders enabled the Southern Utah settlers to survive and thrive in the harsh conditions found in the West. They have left behind lasting achievements, some of which I'll highlight.

Session 242 (2:45 p.m., Friday, September 13)

Title: Both RLDS and LDS Erred in their Method of Presidential Succession by William Russell read by Michael H. Nielsen

Abstract: The choice of Brigham Young as LDS prophet made sense since Hyrum was killed at Carthage and Sidney Rigdon was no longer highly regarded by the saints. And Joseph Smith III was a good choice for the various saints who did not want to follow Brigham to what became Utah. Young Joseph was well suited for the Midwestern Saints who lived among Methodists, Lutherans, Baptists, Catholics, and their neighbors. Giving up Joseph Jr.'s Nauvoo innovations like polygamy, the plurality of gods, baptism for the dead and other temple rituals was a better fit for the Midwestern Saints.

But both churches erred in making that first presidential succession the rule for the future. The RLDS were stuck with the small pickings of male members of one family, while their Utah cousins have been stuck with in many cases very old men. I will explain why both of these systems were a big mistake.

Biographical Sketch: William D. Russell received a BA in religion from Graceland University, an MDiv from Saint Paul School of Theology in Kansas City, and a JD from the University of Iowa at Saint Paul. He has been the President of both the Mormon History Association and the John Whitmer Historical Association. Bill has been the author of at least fifty book reviews and forty articles in the *John Whitmer Historical Association Journal*, the *Mormon Historical Association Journal*, *Sunstone Magazine*, the *Utah Historical Journal*, and the *Christian Century*.

He served on the faculty at Graceland University for forty-one years, 1966–2007, and part-time for ten years thereafter. He taught Introduction to Christianity, Old Testament, New Testament, the History of Christian I and II, RLDS/Community of Christ History, History of Religion in America, History of the American Presidency, History of American Law, Political Parties and Pressure Groups, American Government, Constitutional Law, Criminal Justice, Racism and Discrimination, and History of Women in America.

Title: Beehive Girls and the Priesthood: Reactions to Women's Ordination and Feminism in LDS Church Curriculum in the 1970s and 1980s by Nancy Ross, David J. Howlett

Abstract: A host of studies have focused on The Church of Jesus Christ of Latter-day Saints and the Equal Rights Amendment, showing how the church's opposition to the latter served as a proxy for its stance on feminism and liberal modernity (Bradley, 2005). Martha Sontag Bradley has shown how conservative LDS leaders and conservative BYU scholars saw the ERA as a threat to the all-male priesthood. We want to know if the messages of the memos and letters she cites made it into the formation of young LDS members through official, correlated educational materials about priesthood. To answer this query, we want to examine the manuals in the Prince Collection at UVA related to Beehive Girls. In the 1970s until the recent past, "Beehive Girls" denoted LDS girls ages twelve and thirteen. At this age and coinciding with the general onset of puberty, LDS girls began single-gender education classes in which they were taught a curriculum written explicitly for girls. We theorize, then, that Beehive Girl manuals will be potent sources for understanding what the LDS church was saying (or not saying) about women and the priesthood in the 1970s and 1980s. In particular, we want to know how these sources 1) describe priesthood holders, 2) describe priesthood-specific activities, 3) define manhood, 4) define womanhood, 5) prescribe activities appropriate for women, 5) describe the proper relationship between women and priesthood holders, and 6) evidence the expansion or contraction of women's roles as a result of awareness of expanding roles of women (including ordination) in other traditions.

Biographical Sketch: David J. Howlett is visiting assistant professor of religion at Smith College in Northampton, Massachusetts, and is the author of *Kirtland Temple: The Biography of a Shared Mormon Sacred Space* (University of Illinois Press, 2014) and co-author of *Mormonism: The Basics* (Routledge, 2017). He is the immediate past president of the Mormon History Association and a volunteer church historian for Community of Christ.

Biographical Sketch: Nancy Ross is a department chair and associate professor in the Interdisciplinary Arts and Sciences Department at Utah Tech University, where she has been teaching for eighteen years. Her PhD is in art history, but her current research focuses on the history and sociology of religion. She is an ordained elder in Community of Christ and pastor of the Southern Utah congregation.

Session 243 (2:45 p.m., Friday, September 13)

Title: "Armed Men, Furious Men, With Murder in Their Hearts": The Men Who Killed Joseph and Hyrum Smith—Claims, Accusations, and Pus-filled Wounds by Joseph Johnstun

Abstract: Since the murders of Joseph and Hyrum Smith 180 years ago, many attempts have been made to determine who actually did the deed. Many contemporaries compiled lists of those whom they believed had been a part of the mob that stormed the Hancock County jail or those whom they believed ultimately responsible. Additionally, as years passed, several participants, their families, and associates, revealed their presence. Here, Johnstun reviews the early lists, confessions, claims, and statements, to come up with a new list of most-likely participants.

Biographical Sketch: Joseph Johnstun is an historical analyst from Fort Madison, Iowa. He has been an historical consultant and advisor for numerous publications, projects, and media presentations on historic sites, documents, and artifacts. He is one of the leading scholars on Nauvoo history, and is the expert on the murder of Joseph and Hyrum Smith. He is the director of the Tomb of Joseph Museum in Nauvoo, Illinois.

Title: Did Joseph Smith Really Faint? —The June 25, 1844 Militia Review in Carthage, Illinois by Bryon Andreasen

Abstract: This presentation is a comparative analysis of conflicting nineteenth-century accounts of the militia review when Joseph and Hyrum Smith were paraded before militia members assembled on the public square in Carthage, Illinois, two days before the Smiths were murdered in the Hancock County jail.

An accurate understanding of this event is important for correctly assessing the conduct and motivations of political leaders and militia officers, as well as contrasting moods and tempers among the various militia units assembled from a four-county region during the tragic last weeks of June 1844. It is also important for understanding how Latter-day Saints and their opponents perceived and interpreted events differently based on prejudices and biased assumptions. Finally, it is a cautionary case study in how reconstructing history from conflicting primary sources is fraught with difficulty and uncertainty.

Biographical Sketch: Bryon Andreasen has a JD from Cornell University and a PhD in nineteenth-century American history from the University of Illinois at Urbana–Champaign. He was research historian at the Abraham Lincoln Presidential Library & Museum in Springfield, Illinois; authored the feasibility study on which Congress based legislation creating the Abraham Lincoln National Heritage Area; and edited the *Journal of the Abraham Lincoln Association*. In 2013, he became historical curator at the Church History Museum in Salt Lake City, Utah. He is working on a biography of Illinois pioneers Miner and Abigail Deming. This presentation is a spin-off from that project.

Session 244 (2:45 p.m., Friday, September 13)

Title: Striving to Make Peace with the Mountain Meadows Massacre by LaJean Purcell Carruth

Abstract: How does one seek to make peace with an atrocity, with the effects of many years working and research on sheer horror? Starting in May 2002, I transcribed and proofread the fourteen hundred pages of extant shorthand records from John D. Lee's two trials for his role in the Mountain Meadows Massacre. I presented an account of my descent into PTSD from that work at MHA in June 2024. This paper will be a discussion on my personal efforts to seek peace with the massacre itself and with my work thereon.

Biographical Sketch: LaJean Purcell Carruth is a professional transcriber of documents written in Pitman shorthand, Taylor shorthand, and in the Deseret Alphabet at the Church History Library, Salt Lake City, Utah. She is fascinated (and often frustrated) by anything written in these scripts. She is also an avid weaver; her weaving hangs in historic sites in Harmony, Palmyra, Kirtland, and Nauvoo.

Title: The Influence of Juanita Brooks on Restoration History by Teresa Reber Bell, Sharla Brooks Moody

Abstract: In this session, Juanita Brook's granddaughter and grandniece will present a captivating exploration into her personal life and legacy. Against the backdrop of the newly thriving city of St. George, Brooks played a vital role in nurturing the ragged edge of civilization by ensuring its growth and prosperity through her ability to gather and expose its earliest history. As we delve into her remarkable journey, we will uncover her tireless efforts in research and advocacy, shedding light on her invaluable contributions to the Restoration Movement. We will also explore her unwavering faithfulness and address persistent misconceptions and provide clarity on her enduring legacy.

Biographical Sketch: Teresa Reber Bell is professor of German and second language acquisition at Brigham Young University in Provo, Utah. She has been fascinated by the life of her great-aunt Juanita Brooks since she was a little girl and has followed in Juanita's footsteps to become an educated woman who researches and writes. Her current research focuses on successful language learning and designing language courses to assist students in becoming global citizens. She regularly leads study abroad programs to Vienna, Austria. She's married to Ryan Bell from Tucson, and they have two young adult children.

Biographical Sketch: Sharla Brooks Moody grew up in St. George where she could see the Dixie Sugarloaf from her bedroom window. She was tutored in all things family, and history, by her dad Karl Brooks while either living with, or next door to, her grandma, Juanita. Thanks to her parents and grandparents, she also had a front row seat in the classroom of community service and connection. She graduated from Dixie High, Dixie College and then SUSC (Southern Utah State College) where she followed in the footsteps of her mother and both of her grandmothers by majoring in English. She then taught English as an adjunct at SUU (Southern Utah University) while her husband finished his masters. She is married to Paul Moody and is the mother of four children and five grandchildren. She's passionate about learning, walking long distances, and her faith. In addition to traveling to spend time with family, she loves old music, old people, and old stories and regularly spends time with all three. She has family history in her heart and red dirt between her toes and hopes to pass both of these on to her children and grandchildren.

Session 301 (8:00 a.m., Saturday, September 14)

Title: Playing with the Enlightenment's Shadows: 19th-Century Witchcraft Hysteria in Early Mormon History by Manuel W. Padro

Abstract: Joseph Smith was accused of diabolical and pretended magic throughout his ministry. Operating under the common assumption that the enlightenment ended witchcraft belief and violence, historians of Mormonism have treated these allegations as credible accounts.

By including modern scholarship on witchcraft belief and anti-witchcraft violence during the counter-enlightenment, it is possible to account for religious polemics about magic in the early anti-Mormon narrative. This provides us with a radically different view of how the Smiths may have understood their activities. It also clarifies how Joseph Smith's enemies reimagined those activities in alignment with classical and contemporary beliefs about witchcraft.

Biographical Sketch: Manuel W. Padro (MPH) is an independent scholar with multiple publications in the fields of public health and Mormon studies. He holds an undergraduate degree in behavioral science (anthropology) from Utah Valley University and a masters in public health from the Colorado School of Public Health. Manuel is finishing a manuscript which revisits the origins of anti-Mormon violence. His analysis reveals important missing pieces in the prophet puzzle: the nexus between early Mormon ceremony, acts of witchcraft (as they were imagined by nineteenth-century people) and the tragically real outcomes of the world's first cholera epidemic.

Title: Keep This from Vulgar Eyes: Mormonism's Tradition of Hidden Books by Nicholas S. Literski

Abstract: Mormonism begins with a hidden book. Hidden writings appear in numerous other stories, including The Book of Mormon, the legends of Freemasonry and magical texts. Dr. Literski will discuss early Mormon encounters with hidden books of magic, ranging from ritual books consulted by Joseph Smith's early associates to grimoires carried by early Mormons converts to America. In particular, Dr. Literski will trace the origin and history of a unique grimoire linking early Mormons to pivotal players in the eighteenth and nineteenth century renaissance of magic in Great Britain—a manuscript that ends with "Carefully keep this from Vulgar Eyes."

Biographical Sketch: Nicholas S. Literski, JD, PhD (They/Them) is a professor of Depth Psychology & Creativity at Pacifica Graduate Institute and a professional spiritual guide. Nick holds a PhD in depth psychology with emphasis in Jungian and archetypal studies from Pacifica Graduate Institute, an MA in spiritual guidance from Sofia University, and a JD from the Northern Illinois University College of Law. Their work has been published in multiple professional journals, and they participate regularly in numerous conferences, podcasts, and other scholarly forums. Their book, *Method Infinite: Freemasonry and the Mormon Restoration*, was published by Greg Kofford Books in 2022.

Session 302 (8:00 a.m., Saturday, September 14)

Title: Restoration Eschatologies and their Conceptual Metaphors by Allegra Goldstraß

Abstract: A wealth of unique eschatological conceptions has been brought forth by the various expressions of the so-called Latter Day Saint movement. Even though the term itself may point to a pronounced interest in the "last things," it can be challenging to untangle the nuances concerning teachings dealing with the afterlife, the end of the world, and the connection between those ideas, especially when the vast variation between different expressions of the movement is taken into account.

This paper presents the results of a research project examining the eschatological positions of various Restoration churches in light of their historical development. The analysis of material published by these organizations focuses not only on eschatological teachings per se but also on the manner in which these are discussed. Religions rely on the use of metaphors to create and convey meaning transcending the material world. The application of Conceptual Metaphor theory allows us to identify the known (source) domains used to understand the hereafter. This approach grants access to insights beyond a surface-level comparison of theological and doctrinal positions, unveiling differences and commonalities in the manner the various branches of the Restoration think about postmortal existence and the end of the world.

Biographical Sketch: Allegra Goldstraß holds a BA in archaeology and religious studies. She is currently pursuing an MA in religious studies at the Center of Religious Studies at Ruhr University Bochum, Germany. Her studies focus on the anthropology of religion, eschatology, and the Latter Day Saint movement. Allegra works as a research assistant on the Middle Persian Corpus Dictionary Project, where she has developed an appreciation for the methods of the digital humanities. Outside of her research, she serves as speaker of the student council, where she is involved in a variety of activities, such as the organization of events.

Title: John Tanner Clark and the Enigma of the "One Mighty and Strong" by Cyrus Simper

Abstract: John Tanner Clark's early life, marked by socio-religious and political influences, set the stage for later theological innovations within the Latter-day Saint community. Using Clark as a case study, this work explores broader Mormon fundamentalism, analyzing his writings, patriarchal blessings, census, biographical, and other data to reconstruct the milieu that spurred the movement. The study highlights his intricate ties with figures such as J. W. Musser, Mattias F. Cowley, Daniel Bateman, and Lorin Woolley, uncovering the interplay between personal background and theological innovation, providing new insights into the socio-religious dynamics of the late nineteenth and early twentieth centuries.

Biographical Sketch: Cyrus Simper holds degrees from Brigham Young University–Idaho where he studied sociology and data science. He has experience as an archivist for the Guy H. Musser Archives. He currently leads projects on the early financing of the United Effort Plan and a penitentiary poetry project. His research interests include textile preservation, computer-aided indexing, machine learning, and natural language processing. Notable publications include studies on COVID-19 mental health impacts and Mormon sacred clothing. He will present his research on patriarchal blessings at the SSSR and plans to pursue a PhD in computational social science.

Session 303 (8:00 a.m., Saturday, September 14)

Title: RLDS Reunion Grounds: Change and Continuity by William D. Moore

Abstract: The Reorganized Church of Jesus Christ of Latter Day Saints, commonly called the RLDS, initiated multi-day outdoor reunions for its membership in the final decades of the nineteenth century. By 1981, the church maintained 132 developed grounds which were frequently wooded and almost universally provided access to water, both for recreation and for baptisms.

Largely held during the summer, RLDS reunions became increasingly formalized over the course of the twentieth century, transforming over time from ephemeral campsites to permanent compounds resembling sectarian summer camps. Reunion grounds became essential for enacting and inculcating RLDS identity and ideology as local and regional organizations acquired property throughout the United States and Canada. Like camp meeting groves of Protestant denominations, RLDS reunion grounds evolved to contain tents and other sleeping accommodations, recreational facilities, dining structures, and spaces for worship and religious education.

These compounds have not been adequately documented and interpreted. By drawing upon written records, church publications, historical photographs, and the buildings and landscapes which comprise these institutions, this illustrated, analytic overview seeks to rectify this gap in the historical literature while simultaneously expanding scholarship on Latter Day Saint architecture and contributing to a nuanced history of the American Restorationist movement.

Biographical Sketch: William D. Moore, PhD, is an American studies scholar with a joint appointment as Associate Professor of American material culture in the Department of History of Art and Architecture and the American and New England Studies Program at Boston University. He has an abiding interest in the intersection of built form and systems of religious belief. *Shaker Fever: America's Twentieth Century Fascination with a Communitarian Sect* (University of Massachusetts Press, 2020) is his most recent book.

Title: RLDS Young Adults on Mission: Older Youth Service Corps, 1964-1973 by Katherine Pollock

Abstract: In 1964 the Reorganized Church of Jesus Christ of Latter Day Saints created Older Youth Service Corps (OYSC), a program for youth adults which assigned them on missions across the United States and the world. OYSC was successful with RLDS young adults and growing, but suddenly faded away only after a decade. This presentation shares the following research: the history of OYSC from its inception to its disappearance in the mid-1970s, highlights from several youth adult missions taken during the 1960s and 1970s, statistics about youth adult participation, and OYSC's relationship with the second iteration of young adult missions, World Service Corps (1999–2018).

Biographical Sketch: Katherine Pollock is a MA student at Missouri State University (Springfield, Missouri) in religious studies. She interned with Community of Christ Historic Sites during the summers of 2016–19 and volunteers at archives. She is interested in twentieth century church history and ethnography. Her research on Older Youth Services Corps came from meeting World Service Corps volunteers during her summers at historic sites.

Session 304 (8:00 a.m., Saturday, September 14)

Title: Prelude to the Oregon and Mormon Trails: From the Secret of South Pass in 1813 to the Ultimatum Map of 1838 by Mark Goodmansen

Abstract: At the same time as Joseph Smith returned to Hill Cumorah to see the golden plates in 1826, Jedediah Smith and his party were passing along the Virgin River in this very region of St. George in Mexican Territory. As part of the Ashley Expedition, they rediscovered South Pass in 1825 and explored Nevada, California, and the Oregon Territory before returning to Missouri. Beginning with John Astor's expeditions to Astoria multiple groups followed, giving rise to what became the Oregon and Mormon Trails. In 1836 the famous Washington Irving published the story of Astoria with an important map of the region which was followed two years later by the Ultimatum Map used in disputes with the British regarding the Joint Occupation of Oregon. Earlier, Irving wrote of Captain Bonneville's expedition through South Pass and Oregon.

In this presentation I will be displaying this original book and maps and telling the hidden story of the exploits of a large anti-Mormon Missouri merchant group and their exploits in this Rocky Mountain region, and the partial fulfillment of Joseph Smith's prophecy.

Biographical Sketch: Mark Goodmansen resides in South Jordan, Utah. He graduated cum laude at the University of Utah in accounting, became a certified public accountant, and served as a business and marketing executive for various companies until retiring. Author of *Conspiracy at Car-*

thage–The Plot to Murder Joseph Smith published by Cedar Fort Publishing in 2016; previously presented, "Francis Scott Key's Visit to Nauvoo in 1841 and Its Impact On the Saints in the Region" at the 2017 JWHA conference, "The Independence Missouri Merchants Versus The Saints of the New Jerusalem" at the 2018 JWHA conference, and "The Clay and Ray County Mormon Removal Committees, and the 1835 Clay County, Missouri Memorial to Congress, Calling for a Military. Road to Clay County," at the 2019 JWHA conference. Also, I presented "Massive anticipated economic rewards expected by the federal appointees led to the Utah War and substantially affected the Promontory Point 1869 event," at the 2019 Mormon History Association conference. I will be presenting at the 2024 Mormon History Association conference.

Title: Scandal, Suicide, and Strife in a Small Southern Utah Community by David R. Taylor

Abstract: On June 26, 1867, the *Deseret News* in Salt Lake City, Utah, printed a brief notice: "SUICIDE. —Elder James Lewis writes that John McCleves [McCleve], a young man residing in Harrisburg, Washington County, aged about 22 years, blew his brains out with a rifle, on the 5th inst."

The scandalous story behind this macabre announcement is an unsolved mystery that divided the fledgling pioneering community of Harrisburg, Utah, located about fifteen miles north of St. George. In 1867, it was home to fewer than two hundred inhabitants made up largely of freighters and ranchers. Twenty-five years later, 90 percent of the settlers had abandoned the site.

Further investigation exposes additional details about the circumstances leading to the drastic act and the subsequent impact on the pioneer community; it also reveals insights into complex family and social relationships and the challenge of creating community in the face of an omnipresent struggle for water.

This paper investigates how these decidedly human factors affected the ability to create a godly community in a rural outpost of southern Utah.

Biographical Sketch: David R. Taylor is a manager of product managers in the Church History Department of The Church of Jesus Christ of Latter-day Saints. As an amateur historian, his research interests include the Latter Day Saint experience during the Nauvoo era and early Latter-day Saint settlements in Utah and Arizona. He is the author of "John

A. Taylor (1812–1896): One Man's Journey Across Three Branches of the Restoration," which will be published in the forthcoming Spring/Summer 2024 issue of the *JWHA Journal*.

Session 311 (9:45 a.m., Saturday, September 14)

Title: John Beck's Fabulous Mine: An Outpost in the Tintic Mountains of Early Utah Territory by R. Jean Addams

Abstract: In the years following the settlement of the Brigham Young-led members of the early church to what became the Territory of Utah, leaders often spoke of the Redemption of Zion and the return of the church to Jackson County as revealed to the prophet Joseph Smith. Over time, the LDS Church entered into various businesses and enterprises; certainly, mining ventures were the most speculative. The story of Jesse Knight is, perhaps, the most well known. However, he was not the first church member to look for gold and silver. This presentation will center on Mormon immigrant, John Beck, who staked a mining claim in the Tintic Mountains in the year 1870 and "struck it rich." Of the various mining ventures involving the LDS church or its leaders, the Bullion-Beck mine, and its "consecrated" stock fund was both unique in its arrangement and purpose and controversial in its management of the "consecrated" fund it created.

In 1883, Beck, known as the "Crazy Dutchman," solicited the help of President John Taylor and his First Counselor, George Q. Cannon, in a restructured corporation of his mine in which the three men would be equals. The proposed participation and purpose was confirmed to Taylor by revelation, whereby Beck and Cannon surrendered 60 per cent of their shares, as did Taylor, into a "consecrated" stock fund. The specified purpose of the fund was for the building of the "Jackson County Temple and ... the Redemption of Zion" and a return of the LDS church to Jackson County.

In 1904 the LDS church re-acquired 20 acres of the original Temple Lot purchased in 1831 by Edward Partridge at Joseph Smith's request. The money used for this repurchase came from a fund simply labeled: "Jackson County Temple and Redemption of Zion."

Biographical Sketch: R. Jean Addams is a lifetime Mormon History enthusiast, independent historian, and author. He and his wife Liz reside in Woodinville, Washington. He holds a BS in accounting and an MBA from the University of Utah. Addams has presented and published several articles dealing with the "Redemption of Zion" and related topics. He is the author of *Upon the Temple Lot: The Church of Christ's Quest to Build the House of the Lord* (John Whitmer Books, 2010). Addams is a past president of the John Whitmer Historical Association, and a member of the Mormon History Association, and the Missouri Mormon Frontier Foundation. His other interests include family and fishing.

Title: "Some Friends and Also Brethren": Religious "Outposts" in the Western Missouri Borderlands, 1825–1835 by Sherilyn Farnes

Abstract: Members of the Restoration group founded by Joseph Smith began moving in large numbers to Independence, Missouri, and the surrounding areas in Jackson County in 1831. While they were targeted for their religious beliefs, there were a surprisingly large number of religious groups also establishing churches, missions, and communities of believers in the region at the time. Catholics, Methodists, Baptists, Church of Christ, those practicing indigenous religions, and others gathered in this region.

My paper will provide a brief overview of the religious climate in the region in the late 1820s and early 1830s, including the interactions of those of different faiths with each other. It will also touch on the interplay between religion and government in multiple ways, including the expulsion of the Church of Christ and religious conflicts between Indian Agents in the region. This paper will not only help situate the early Church of Christ settlers in religious context, but also broaden the scholarship on religion in the western Missouri borderlands during the early Jacksonian Era to better understand the religious nature of the region.

Biographical Sketch: Sherilyn Farnes earned her BA and MA from Brigham Young University and her PhD from Texas Christian University in US history. Her scholarly publications and presentations have focused on Latter-day Saint, women's, and early American religious history. She teaches part time in BYU religious education and has worked with the Joseph Smith Papers Project and on the writing team of *Saints: The Story of the Church of Jesus Christ in the Latter Days*. Her dissertation analyzed the interactions of Shawnee, Delaware, Osage, Latter-day Saints, French fur traders, missionaries, and other settlers in the western Missouri borderlands during the Jacksonian Era.

Session 312 (9:45 a.m., Saturday, September 14)

Title: Early Mormon Women and the Word of Wisdom by Sherrie Gavin

Abstract: As early as 1833, notable food restrictions were declared as a part of the fledgling Mormon tradition. The "Word of Wisdom" is the phrase used to define this cannon in the 89th section of what would become known as the Doctrine and Covenants; it is commonly recognized in modern terms as the abstinence of tobacco, coffee, tea, and alcohol, and the admonition to eat grains and to eat meat "sparingly." Whilst current scholarly work exists on the history, administration, and development of the Word of Wisdom, very little of this research is aimed at addressing the gender-related experiences of Mormon women with this policy and its fluctuating adherence. Using qualitative analysis of Mormon women's food records, this paper aims to analyze Mormon women's food and medicinal preparations specifically addressing the uses of tobacco, coffee, tea, alcohol and meat, as well as the everyday uses of these products in the kitchens of Mormon women. In doing so, we are better able to understand the experiences of Mormon women on a more intimate level, in the domain in which women were obligated to reign: the kitchen.

Biographical Sketch: Sherrie Gavin is a PhD Candidate at the University of New England, Australia with an interest in the multidisciplinary fields of food studies, gender studies, and religious studies. She has previously been published in the *Journal of Mormon History* and her forthcoming memoir; *Turning Pink* will be released by BCC press in April 2025.

Title: Sarah Maria Mousley Cannon: Making Peace with "the days of our poverty" by Marian Peck Rees

Abstract: Sarah Maria Mousley was born into a well-to-do family in Centerville, Delaware, in 1828. After most of the Mousley family joined The Church of Jesus Christ of Latter-day Saints, Father Titus Mousley, who never joined the church, made a life-changing decision to move the family to Utah. Sarah Maria became the first wife of Angus M. Cannon.

Angus and Sarah were called to go to St. George on the "Cotton Mission," where she gave birth in a wagon box to the "the first white child born in St. George."

Sarah's life in Utah was much different than it would have been in Delaware. But she was a hard-working woman who made the best of her circumstances. In her last years, she was heard to say, "We had to struggle, we worked hard, but we had good health, and strength, courage and brains, and no one so equipped is ever poor."

Biographical Sketch: Marian Peck Rees has a BS degree from the University of Utah in elementary education. She does not claim to be a historian either by training or experience. She is, however, very interested in history, especially as that history relates to Mormonism, and her own Mormon ancestors.

After spending her adult life raising five children and teaching young children in the public schools, Marian has spent a good deal of her retirement learning about the lives of her ancestors, especially the women.

Marian grew up in the neighborhood where her mother, grandmother, and two of her great-grandmothers lived. This proximity added to her interest in their lives. Sarah Maria Mousley was one of those great-grandmothers.

Session 313 (9:45 a.m., Saturday, September 14)

Title: Reconciliation with First Nations Peoples/Native Americans on the Eve of the Book of Mormon's Bicentennial by John C. Hamer

Abstract: Meeting from 2008 to 2015, the official Truth and Reconciliation Commission of Canada heard testimony and gathered evidence documenting the treatment of the indigenous peoples of North America by Settler governments and institutions, including churches. The report concluded that attacks on First Nations' languages and traditions amounted to "cultural genocide," and issued a call to actively pursue reconciliation going forward.

The Latter Day Saint movement began with the publication of the Book of Mormon, a well-intentioned text that hoped to write the Americas and native peoples into the biblical narrative. While the text does not escape the early nineteenth-century racist paradigm in which it was composed, the Book of Mormon sought to bring native peoples to Christ and endow them with a choice biblical role as heirs of ancient Israel.

Leaving the intentions of our forebearers aside, in the twenty-first century we have the perspective to see that by assigning a fictional biblical narrative to native peoples, the Book of Mormon effectively denies the true history and culture of First Nations peoples and in this way contributed to the cultural genocide committed by the broader Setter community.

In keeping with the Truth and Reconciliation Commission's call to churches to acknowledge past actions, members of Community of Christ in Canada are working to share in dialogue with First Nations partners, in order to compose a suitable acknowledgement and apology for past teaching (in error) that this book of our scriptural canon was a literal history of the natives. This presentation will outline our plans in advance of the 2030 bicentennial.

Biographical Sketch: John C. Hamer is a past president, past executive director, and lifetime member of JWHA. John serves as pastor of Community of Christ's downtown Toronto Congregation of the church's largest online ministry. Every Tuesday, John lectures on a wide variety of topics related to history, theology, and philosophy on the Centre Place YouTube channel, which now has sixty-seven subscribers and eleven million views.

Title: Alex Joseph and Other Lesser-known Latter-day Prophets of Southern Utah by Mike LeCheminant

Abstract: This presentation will discuss four prophets in the Latter Day Saint tradition with connections to Southern Utah. Alex Joseph, along with his wives and followers, moved to a ghost town in the 1970s which he renamed Big Water. He was the leader of the Church of Jesus Christ in Solemn Assembly, as well as a theo-political organization called the Confederate Nations of Israel. Leland Freeborn founded the Kingdom of God in Parowan. One of his followers, Samuel Schaffer, founded the Church of the Diamond, the Patriarchal Order of the Church of Christ, and the Knights of the Crystal Blade. David Wood is the prophet of the Kingdom of Elohim, an online church in St. George. Each of these small groups show the variety of religious experience found in the divergent paths of the restoration.

Biographical Sketch: Mike LeCheminant has received degrees in biology, dentistry, and endodontics from Brigham Young University, the University of Louisville, and the University of Southern California, and he is currently a part-time history student at Sam Houston State University. He has a wife, seven children, and five dogs, and he practices dentistry in Houston, Texas, specializing in root canals.

Panel 314 (9:45 a.m., Saturday, September 14)

Title: New American Zion: Benjamin E. Park's American Zion a New History of Mormonism by Benjamin E. Park, David J. Howlett, Nancy Ross, Matthew Harris

Abstract: This proposed session features three noted scholars, namely Professors, David J. Howlett, Matthew Harris and Nancy Ross interacting with Professor Benjamin E. Park relative to his recently published, widely publicized *American Zion: A New History of Mormonism.*

The format would be as follows: Each of the three scholars would take turns in providing an overview of Park's *American Zion* in terms of its strengths, weaknesses, and of the volume's significance/contributions to the overall field of Restoration/Mormon Studies.

Biographical Sketch: Benjamin E. Park received his PhD in history from the University of Cambridge and is an associate professor at Sam Houston State University. He is co-editor of *Mormon Studies Review*, editor of Blackwell's *A Companion to American Religious History*, and author or editor of five books, including *Kingdom of Nauvoo: The Rise and Fall of a Religious Empire on the American Frontier*. His most recent book is *American Zion: A New History of Mormonism.*

Biographical Sketch: David J. Howlett is visiting assistant professor of religion at Smith College in Northampton, Massachusetts, and is the author of *Kirtland Temple: The Biography of a Shared Mormon Sacred Space* (University of Illinois Press, 2014) and co-author of *Mormonism: The Basics* (Routledge, 2017). He is the immediate past-president of the Mormon History Association and a volunteer church historian for Community of Christ.

Biographical Sketch: Nancy Ross is a department chair and associate professor in the Interdisciplinary Arts and Sciences Department at Utah Tech University, where she has been teaching for eighteen years. Her PhD is in art history, but her current research focuses on the history and sociology of religion. She is an ordained elder in Community of Christ and pastor of the Southern Utah congregation.

Biographical Sketch: Matthew Harris is a professor of history at Colorado State University–Pueblo. He earned his BA and MA in history from Brigham Young University and his MPhil and PhD, also in history, from the Maxwell School of Citizenship and Public Affairs at Syracuse University. He is the author and/or editor of numerous books, including most recently *Second-Class Saints: Black Mormons and the Struggle for Racial Equality* (Oxford University Press, 2024) and *Watchman on the Tower: Ezra Taft Benson and the Making of the Mormon Right* (University of Utah Press, 2020). An award-winning teacher, he has won his university's top awards for teaching, research, and service. His work has been featured on C-SPAN, Longreads, the Religious News Service, and dozens of news and social media outlets. He is the president elect of the John Whitmer Historical Association.

Panel 321 (11:00 a.m., Saturday, September 14)

Title: Summers Well Spent: Reminiscing on Alma Blair and the Internship Program at Nauvoo and Kirtland by Barbara Walden, Christine Blythe, Christopher Elyse Blythe, Katherine Pollock, Magen Edvalson

Abstract: With the passing of its eponymous benefactor in 2023 and the sale of the Kirtland and Nauvoo historic sites, the Community of Christ's Alma Blair Internship Program (formerly known as the Museum Management Internship Program) is on the brink of a major shift in how it involves young adults in Restoration studies. Interns will no longer offer tours of historic sites, but the Historic Sites Foundation that sponsors the program will continue to provide opportunities for students. What will this reimaging look like? How will Community of Christ young adults engage with church history and preservation? Join a round table discussion with Community of Christ Historic Sites Foundation Director Barbara Walden, and former historic sites interns Chris and Christine Blythe, Katherine Pollock, and Magen Edvalson, as they share some of Alma's legacy, reminisce about their summers as interns, and talk about their hopes for the future of the program.

Biographical Sketch: Barbara Walden earned a BA in history from Graceland University and an MA in museum studies from the Cooperstown Graduate Program (SUNY Oneonta). Following graduate school, Barbara served as the site director of the Kirtland Temple from 2002–09. Today, she is the executive director of the Community of Christ Historic Sites Foundation, faculty member at the Community of Christ Seminary, and one of three church historians for Community of Christ. Barbara served as the John Whitmer Historical Association president from 2007–08 and on the board of directors for both the Mormon History Association and the John Whitmer Historical Association.

Biographical Sketch: Christine Elyse Blythe earned her MA in folklore from Memorial University of Newfoundland and a BA in religious studies from Utah State University. She is co-editor of *Open Canon: Scriptures of the Latter Day Saint Tradition* (University of Utah, 2022), co-president of the Folklore Society of Utah and co-host of the podcast Angels and Seerstones a Latter-day Saint Folklore Podcast. In 2022 Christine left her position as curator of the William A. Wilson Folklore Archives at Brigham Young University's L. Tom Perry Special Collections for her current position as the Executive Director of Mormon History Association

Biographical Sketch: Magen Edvalson serves as the coordinator for the Oral History Project of Community of Christ and sits as a board member of JWHA. They hold a bachelor's degree in theatre from the University of Utah and a master's degree in English with an emphasis in folklore from Utah State University. Their research interests include intersecting folk identities in Restoration communities, ex-Mormon folklore, and Community of Christ culture. They currently reside in Silverton, Oregon with their spouse.

Biographical Sketch: Christopher James Blythe is an assistant professor of folklore and Latter-day Saint literature at Brigham Young University. He is the author of *Terrible Revolution: Latter-day Saints and the American Apocalypse* (Oxford, 2020) and co-editor of *Open Canon: Scriptures of the Latter Day Saint Tradition* (Utah, 2022). Christopher Blythe also hosts the podcast, Angels and Seerstones with his wife, Christine.

Biographical Sketch: Katherine Pollock is a MA student at Missouri State University (Springfield, Missouri) in religious studies. She interned with Community of Christ Historic Sites during the summers of 2016–19 and volunteers at archives. She is interested in twentieth century church history and ethnography. Her research on Older Youth Services Corps came from meeting World Service Corps volunteers during her summers at historic sites.

Session 322 (11:00 a.m., Saturday, September 14)

Title: Rebecca Wheeler Wright by Barbara Morgan Gardner

Abstract: Rebecca Wheeler Wright, wife of Jonathan Calkins Wright, joined the Church of Jesus Christ in 1843 with her husband Jonathan Calkins Wright in Nauvoo, Illinois. Their home was built just doors down from Hyrum Smith and the Red Brick Store. Although Jonathan arrived in Utah in 1848, eventually serving as a mayor in Brigham City and counselor to Lorenzo Snow and becoming a polygamist with multiple wives and children to tell his story, Rebecca died near Winter Quarter's with an unmarked grave, and no published material to remember her life and sacrifice. This paper and presentation seeks to bring her story to life using her personal diary, letters, and family history.

As the Jonathan and Rebecca Wheeler home has been owned for years by the Community of Christ church, I have worked with Lach Mackay in "outpost" situations to learn more about this home and my ancestors in context of Nauvoo history. Over the years I have interviewed descendants of Rebecca Wheeler Wright and Jonathan Çalkins Wright, collected pictures, family heirlooms, and significant historical documents. Her story, that of a silent voice, is waiting and ready to be told!

Biographical Sketch: Barbara Morgan Gardner is a professor of Church History and Doctrine at BYU. She recently created a course entitled "Women of Covenant Leadership." This topic has become her passion both in terms of research, writing, teaching and mentoring. She is the author of the *Priesthood Power of Women in the Temple, Church and Family*. She is the host of "Grounded," a new by women for women scripture podcast and co-hosts an Instagram Live "Walk with Him," with Elaine Dalton. She serves as the LDS Chaplain-at-large in higher education. Barbara is married to Dustin Gardner and they have two children.

Title: The Women of the "Texas Epidemic"; Come to Pine Valley by Melvin C. Johnson

Abstract: Members of the Lyman Wight Colony, formerly of the Church of Jesus Christ of Latter-day Saints, had searched from the early 1850s for a new home on the frontier. One group of sixty people, including former Wightites and a few scattered families of the Mormon Restoration had reunited in 1856 with the LDS church in Utah Territory and Southern Utah in the 1850s and 1860s, particularly in Pine Valley. It will examine the challenges the women encountered, endured, and overcame, including marriages, death of children, and the weight of being polygamous spouses. The presentation will conclude with the RLDS conversion of the Hawley families and their immigration to Iowa to join their relatives in the Reorganization.

Biographical Sketch: Melvin C. Johnson is an independent historian and retired college professor, writer, and speaker who pursues subjects dealing with the Texas Hill country before and in the Civil War, and the intersection of Western America and Mormonism. His work won the Smith-Pettit Best Book Award (2007) for *Polygamy on the Pedernales: Lyman Wight's Mormon Village in Antebellum Texas*; the Greg Kofford Best Theological Article (2017); for "John Hawley: His LDS Mission to Iowa and Eventual RLDS Conversion," *John Whitmer Historical Association Journal*; and the Greg Kofford Alma Blair Best Biography for the *Life and Times of John Pierce Hawley: A Mormon Ulysses of the American West* (2019). Mel and Halli, his wife, live in Mesquite, Nevada.

Session 323 (11:00 a.m., Saturday, September 14)

Title: The Revelations of Heber C. Kimball by Clair Barrus

Abstract: Heber C. Kimball recorded over two dozen revelations in his journal and in the back of a book titled "H. C. Kimballs Memorandum." Five revelations were recorded in his journal beginning in early June 1844 through January 1845. His memorandum book contains twenty-one revelations, or portions of thereof, received between 1852 and 1864. Some of them are secondary versions—providing clues how revelation evolved during his writing process. Some were apparently removed from the memorandum book because they were too personal or controversial—and are unavailable for research. Some were received through a divining rod given to him by Joseph Smith.

Biographical Sketch: Clair Barrus has published in the *Journal of Mormon History, John Whitmer Historical Association Journal,* and has a chapter on the Plural Marriage Revelations of Joseph Smith in the recently published *Secret Covenants: New insights on early Mormon Polygamy*. Clair also manages TodayInMormonhistory.com.

Title: The End Times According to Latter Day Saint Joseph Smith Senior by H. Michael Marquardt

Abstract: Joseph Smith Senior was ordained to the office of Patriarch in the early Latter Day Saint (Mormon) movement. Smith is the father of Mormonism's founder Joseph Smith Junior. In Joseph Smith Senior's calling he pronounced blessings on church members. He made predictions including how long a person may live, if they would be living at the winding up scene at the Second Coming of Jesus Christ, the return of the ten lost tribes, and the possibility of being among the 144,000 faithful. This historical presentation will be based upon the recorded patriarchal blessings for the time period of 1834–40.

Biographical Sketch: H. Michael Marquardt is an independent historian and research consultant. He is the compiler of *Early Patriarchal Blessings of The Church of Jesus Christ of Latter-day Saints* (Smith-Pettit Foundation, 2007) and *Later Patriarchal Blessings of The Church of Jesus Christ of Latter-day Saints* (Smith-Pettit Foundation, 2012) and the author of *The Four Gospels According to Joseph Smith* (Xulon Press, 2007); *Joseph Smith's 1828-1843 Revelations* (Xulon Press, 2013); *The Rise of Mormonism: 1816-1844* (2nd ed., Xulon Press, 2013) and co-author with William Shepard of *Lost Apostles: Forgotten Members of Mormonism's Original Quorum of Twelve* (Signature Books, 2014).

Session 324 (11:00 a.m., Saturday, September 14)

Title: Joseph Hyrum Grant, Heber J. Grant, and the Passing of LDS Plural Marriage by Todd Compton

Abstract: In his youth, Heber J. Grant was a dedicated supporter of polygamy, and he married two plural wives in 1884. He also performed two post-Manifesto marriages, in 1897. His brother, Joseph Hyrum Grant, Stake President of the Davis Stake, participated in a plural marriage two years after the Manifesto. One of Joseph Hyrum's counselors in the Stake Presidency, James Eldredge, and his local bishop, Dan Muir, participated in plural marriages two years after the Second Manifesto, in 1906. Yet two of Heber J. Grant's wives died, and he was a monogamist after 1909. During his term as church president, he became widely known for requiring monogamy in the LDS Church, and actively disciplined new polygamists.

Biographical Sketch: Todd Compton has written books and articles on Mormon polygamy, *In Sacred Loneliness: The Plural Wives of Joseph Smith* (1997), *In Sacred Loneliness: the Documents* (2022), and, with Charles Hatch, *A Widow's Tale: The 1884–1896 Diary of Helen Mar Kimball Whitney* (2003). He has also written articles and books related to southern Utah, such as *A Frontier Life: Jacob Hamblin, Explorer and Indian Missionary* (2013). He is now working on a biography of Navajo leader Ganado Mucho. He lives in the Bay Area in California with his wife and two children.

Title: Heber Bennion: Heber J. Grant's Rogue Brother-in-Law by Newell G. Bringhurst

Abstract: This proposed paper explores the extraordinary odyssey of Heber Bennion, who, while serving as bishop of the Taylorsville ward, entered into post-Manifesto polygamy, marrying two plural wives; doing this, despite being the brother-in-law of LDS church president Heber J. Grant. Bennion, through the second of his plural wives, fathered eight children, which in addition to the ten that he had with his first wife, made for unusually complex family dynamics.

Initially, Bennion managed to keep his plural marriages secret from everyone, except for close family members. However, following his release as Taylorsville bishop, he publicly expressed strong support for plural marriage, as essential church doctrine; doing so through a series of published works—ultimately embraced by the fledgling Mormon Fundamentalist movement. Despite this, Bennion remained a mainstream Latter-day Saint. At the time of his death in 1932, he was accorded a traditional LDS funeral held at the Taylorsville Ward he had once presided over—a service attended by none other than President Heber J. Grant!

Biographical Sketch: Newell G. Bringhurst is an independent scholar and Professor Emeritus of History and Political Science at College of the Sequoias in Visalia California. He is the author/editor of fifteen books published since 1981. His most recent is *Harold B. Lee: Life and Thought* (2021). He has served as president of both the Mormon History Association (1999–2000) and of the John Whitmer Historical Association (2005–06). He is also the recipient of the Leonard J. Arrington Award (2021) from the Mormon History Association.

Title: Hugh B. Brown confronts Polygamy within his own Family by Matthew Harris

Abstract: Polygamy played a pivotal role in Mormon apostle Hugh B. Brown's life. Though he didn't engage in the practice himself, it hovered over him throughout his life, affecting both his LDS church ministry and his private life.

This paper will examine four distinct incidents in Brown's life that shaped his views of this salient Mormon practice. The first was when he returned home from his LDS mission in 1905, some fifteen years after church president Wilford Woodruff announced a revelation discontinuing the practice. Upon his return to Canada, church apostle John W. Taylor urged the newly returned missionary to engage in polygamy. The next incident occurred in the 1920s when Brown presided over the Granite Stake in Salt Lake City. Church president Heber J. Grant asked him to purge his stake membership rolls of defiant individuals who continued the practice; and the president also asked him to craft legislation that would criminalize polygamy. A decade later polygamy hit Brown personally when his son-in-law, Rulon Jeffs, announced that he had intended to take a second wife, which ultimately led to the end of his marriage to Brown's daughter. And finally, in 1958, when Brown was a member of the Quorum of the Twelve Apostles, church president David O. McKay dispatched him to France to deal with a crisis regarding Mormon missionaries who were teaching that polygamy was divine will.

Drawing on never-before-seen sources, which include letters, diaries, and meeting minutes, this presentation will trace how polygamy defined Brown's church ministry and made him a trusted adviser to three church presidents.

Biographical Sketch: Matthew Harris is a professor of history at Colorado State University–Pueblo. He earned his BA and MA in history from Brigham Young University and his MPhil and PhD, also in history, from the Maxwell School of Citizenship and Public Affairs at Syracuse University. He is the author and/or editor of numerous books, including most recently *Second-Class Saints: Black Mormons and the Struggle for Racial Equality* (Oxford University Press, 2024) and *Watchman on the Tower: Ezra Taft Benson and the Making of the Mormon Right* (University of Utah Press, 2020). An award-winning teacher, he has won his university's top awards for teaching, research, and service. His work has been featured on C-SPAN, Longreads, the Religious News Service, and dozens of news and social media outlets. He is the president elect of the John Whitmer Historical Association.

Session 331 Presidential Banquet & Address (6:30 p.m., Saturday, September 14)

Title: Rupture and Reconciliation: Smith Family Interactions with Mountain Saints in the Midwest, 1846–1900

Abstract: In a matter of just four years, from 1840–44, the family of the Joseph Sr. and Lucy Mack Smith was reduced by half, culminating in the deaths of Joseph, Hyrum, and Samuel during that fateful summer of 1844. Those losses had a marked impact on surviving Smith family members and ushered in a new era for the family, now outnumbered by the surviving female members of the family. This presentation will explore the psychological implications of those losses on the family, surviving family member's attitude toward succession, and their decision to remain in the Midwest. It will then highlight interactions that occurred in the Midwest between the Smith family and their relatives and Saints who had gone west during the second half of the nineteenth century. Finally, it will explore the implications of those interactions and the Smith family's affiliation with the RLDS church, and the persisting challenges of being a Smith in Illinois.

Biographical Sketch: Kyle R. Walker was raised in Ashland, Oregon and Logandale, Nevada. He received his PhD in Marriage and Family Therapy from Brigham Young University (2001) and works as an administrator in the Counseling Center at BYU-Idaho. His research has primarily focused on relationships in restoration history. His doctoral dissertation focused on the family dynamics of the restoration's first family. He is the editor of *United by Faith: The Joseph Sr. and Lucy Mack Smith Family*, and the award-winning biography *William B. Smith: In the Shadow of the Prophet*. Just this summer he published his latest book, *Sister to the Prophet: The Life of Katharine Smith Salisbury*. He is married to Daylene Wilson, and they are the parents of four sons and one daughter.

Hymn Fest (9:00 a.m., Sunday, September 15)

Title: Hymn Fest by Brian C. Hales

Abstract: This year is complete with songs from not only the 1835 hymnal, but also the Strangite, Cutlerite, Community of Christ, and Latter-day Saint traditions, with two favorites of Mormon Fundamentalists never before included in our hymn fests. Don't miss it!

Biographical Sketch: Brian C. Hales is the author or co-author of seven books dealing with plural marriage—most notably the three-volume, *Joseph Smith's Polygamy: History and Theology* (Greg Kofford Books, 2013) Presently, Brian is working on two book-length manuscripts dealing with Joseph Smith's treasure seeking and the authorship of the Book of Mormon. He served a mission to Venezuela for The Church of Jesus Christ of Latter-day Saints and sang with the Mormon Tabernacle Choir for fourteen years. Brian is also past president of the Utah Medical Association (2013) and the John Whitmer Historical Association (2015).

Who can forget Lachlan Mackay's Presidential Address at our 2014 annual conference in Lamoni, Iowa? But ten years later we can still benefit from rereading it as a useful reminder of why we exist as an organization. If we can't use our interest in history to highlight the values and issues that are important to us, what do we hope to accomplish through our work? Since this year's conference addresses the theme of peace, it is a great opportunity to share the address again. It gives us the chance to ponder our organization, what we hope to accomplish through our membership, and how we can use the historian's craft to create a better world.

A Peace Gene Isolated: Joseph Smith III

Lachlan Mackay

September 27, 2014

From an anonymous US Artillery officer writing from the City of Nauvoo, May 8, 1842:

> Yesterday was a great day among the Mormons. Their legion, to the number of two thousand men, was paraded ... and certainly made a very noble and imposing appearance. The evolutions of the troops ... would do honour [*sic*] to any body of armed militia in any of the states, and approximates very closely to our regular forces ... It is true they are part of the militia of the state of Illinois ... but then there are no troops in the states like them in point of enthusiasm and warlike aspect, yea, warlike character. Before many years this legion will be twenty, and perhaps fifty thousand strong, and still augmenting. ...These Mormons are accumulating like a snowball rolling down an inclined plane, which in the end becomes an avalanche ... They have appointed your namesake, Capt. Bennett ... and I am assured that he is now under pay, derived from the titheings [*sic*] of this warlike people. I have seen his plans for fortifying Nauvoo ... I arrived here incog., on the 1st instant, and from the great preparation for the military parade, was induced to stay to see the turnout, which I confess, has astonished and filled me with fears for future consequences. The Mormons, it is true, are now peaceable, but the lion is asleep. Take care, and don't rouse him.[1]

1. *Latter-Day Saints' Millennial Star* (September 1842): 83–84.

How is it that Community of Christ, one branch on the family tree of this "warlike people," ended up with "Pursue Peace on Earth" as a mission initiative, "Pursuit of Peace (Shalom)" as an enduring principle, and with a temple built on a portion of the 1830s temple lot in Jackson County, Missouri, designated as an "Ensign of Peace" and dedicated to the pursuit of peace? How could a people captured by the spirit of militarism in the nineteenth century become so intently focused on peace in the twenty-first century?

Richard Howard, in his 1999 Sterling McMurrin lecture (since renamed the Richard Howard Lecture) "The Quest for Traces of a Peace Gene in Restoration History," began to ask that question in response to comments like one from a colleague who said, "Peace Church? It'll never happen. We cannot possibly be something we've never been before." Informed by the *Oxford Universal Dictionary*, Howard defined peace in his lecture not just as public order and security; but also as inner, personal calmness; a state of friendliness & unity; and a condition in which peace, justice and love prevail—and I shall draw on this same broad definition.[2] I remember sitting in the lodge at Camp Doniphan listening to Dick's talk, and the impression eventually developed within me that the RLDS/Community of Christ emphasis on peace was an expression of the 1960s culture of peace and love (which I knew nothing about since I wasn't born until 1965) and was not in fact rooted in the Restoration.

However, with my 2007 move from Kirtland to Nauvoo and the Joseph Smith Historic Site, I have had the opportunity to become much more familiar with Joseph Smith III. And the more I learn of his story, the more I have become convinced that my focus on the 1960s was off by more than a century. D. Michael Quinn pointed out in his *The Mormon Hierarchy: Origins of Power* that there were significant expressions of peacemaking and even pacifism in the earliest years of the church, and young Joseph III inherited that legacy. In July 1833, church members in Jackson County, Missouri, had initially refused to fight back when attacked or even to speak of revenge. According to John Corrill, "up to this time the Mormons had not so much as lifted a finger, even in their own defense, so tenacious were they for the precepts of the gospel,—'turn the other cheek.'"[3] Quinn points out that the Latter Day Saints also refrained from retaliating following a second attack in October and a third in November when a church gristmill was destroyed. After turning the other cheek three times, church members did respond to a fourth attack, this time on the Big Blue River, by fighting back, much to the surprise of the Missourians.[4]

2. Richard P. Howard, "The Quest for Traces of a Peace Gene in Restoration History," *John Whitmer Historical Association Journal* 23 (2003): 45, 48–50.

3. Quoted in D. Michael Quinn, *The Mormon Hierarchy: Origins of Power* (Salt Lake City: Signature Books in association with Smith Research Associates, 1994), 82.

4. Ibid., 82–84.

Quinn argues that this pattern of turning the other cheek was inspired initially by the example of Joseph Smith Jr. and Sidney Rigdon following their tarring and feathering in Hiram, Ohio, and then by the revelation that would become section 95 (LDS 98) of the Doctrine and Covenants. After calling on the Lord's people to "renounce war and proclaim peace" in Doctrine and Covenants 95:3d, the revelation continued:

> if men will smite you, or your families, once, and ye bear it patiently and revile not against them, neither seek revenge, ye shall be rewarded; but if ye bear it not patiently, it shall be accounted unto you as being meted out a just measure unto you.
>
> And again, if your enemy shall smite you the second time, and you revile not against your enemy, and bear it patiently, your reward shall be an hundredfold.
>
> And again, if he shall smite you the third time, and ye bear it patiently, your reward shall be doubled unto you fourfold;
>
> and these three testimonies shall stand against your enemy, if he repent not, and shall not be blotted out.
>
> And now, verily I say unto you, If that enemy shall escape my vengeance that he be not brought into judgment before me, then ye shall see to it, that ye warn him in my name that he come no more upon you, neither upon your family, even your children's children unto the third and fourth generation;
>
> and then if he shall come upon you, or your children, or your children's children unto the third and fourth generation, I have delivered thine enemy into thine hands, and then if thou wilt spare him thou shalt be rewarded for thy righteousness; and also thy children and thy children's children unto the third and fourth generation;
>
> nevertheless thine enemy is in thine hands, and if thou reward him according to his works, thou art justified, if he has sought thy life, and thy life is endangered by him; thine enemy is in thine hands, and thou art justified. (D&C 95:5a–f)

A violent response to an attack could only be justified after turning the other cheek three times, and even then, "if thou wilt spare him (the attacker) though shalt be rewarded for thy righteousness." Verses 6:b–d of section 95 clarifies, as Quinn points out, that Latter Day Saints "were required to obey divine rule, not secular rule, regarding war and militarism."[5]

> And again, this is the law that I gave unto mine ancients, that they should not go out unto battle against any nation, kindred, tongue, or people, save I, the Lord, commanded them.
>
> And if any nation, tongue, or people should proclaim war against them, they should first lift a standard of peace unto that people, nation, or tongue,
>
> and if that people did not accept the offering of peace, neither the second nor the third time, they should bring these testimonies before the Lord;

5. Ibid., 83. Also Book of Doctrine and Covenants (Independence, MO: Herald Publishing House, 2007), section 95:6b-d

> then, I, the Lord, would give unto them a commandment, and justify them in going out to battle against that nation, tongue, or people,

They could fight back only after lifting up a standard of peace three times, being rejected three times, prayerfully asking for permission to fight, and being commanded by the Lord to proceed.

Doctrine and Covenants 100:3d (LDS 103) provided that commandment, calling for the "redemption of Zion" (Independence, Missouri) by power. Thus, with a commandment in place to use force, the Army of Israel (so-called Zion's Camp) was soon marching on Jackson County with Joseph Smith Jr. leading as commander-in-chief. With the failure of Zion's Camp to retake Independence in June of 1834, the focus returned to peacemaking:

> And again, I say unto you, Sue for peace, not only the people that have smitten you, but also to all people; and lift up an ensign of peace, and make a proclamation for peace unto the ends of the earth; and make proposals for peace, unto those who have smitten you, according to the voice of the Spirit which is in you, and all things shall work together for your good.[6]

This call to pursue peace would later be forgotten by many of the Latter Day Saints when political and cultural differences spiraled out of control in what would become the 1838 Mormon War. The conflict would leave deep and lasting scars as skirmishes became battles to trigger a massacre and an extermination order which, as Alex Baugh has pointed out, meant to forcibly remove vs. kill.[7] The events culminated in the siege and surrender of Far West with Joseph Smith Jr. court martialed and sentenced to death. This action I had understood to be illegal, but apparently the question was not settled until the 1866 *ex parte* Milligan ruling by the US Supreme Court.[8] Despite Alexander Doniphan's intercession on his behalf, Smith remained imprisoned as his followers fled across northern Missouri to the sanctuary of Quincy, Illinois, in the winter of 1839.

My own time in Nauvoo has convinced me that any hope of a peace gene becoming dominant among the Latter Day Saints had been precluded by the trauma of the Far West period. As I struggled to make sense of what often seemed to be overreactions to perceived threats by Smith and his followers in Nauvoo, I became personally acquainted with someone who had developed post-traumatic stress disorder from

6. Doctrine and Covenants, section 102:11a–c. The term "ensign of peace" would later be adopted as the favorite descriptor of the Community of Christ's temple dedicated in Independence, Missouri, in 1994.

7. Heather M. Seferovich, "Extermination Order Not Believed to be 'Death Sentence,'" *Deseret News*, September 16, 2008, http://www.deseretnews.com/article/705381893/Extermination-Order-not-believed-to-be-death-sentence.html?pg=a.

8. US Supreme Court, "Ex parte Milligan, 71 U.S. 4 Wall. 2 2 (1866)," Justia.com, https://supreme.justia.com/cases/federal/us/71/2/case.html.

performing extended historical work relating to a nineteenth-century tragedy. In a kind of personal epiphany, it suddenly occurred to me that those who lived through the horrors of the Far West period must also have been deeply traumatized by their experiences.

I believe that the "Myth of Persecuted Innocence,"[9] as discussed by Roger Launius and John Hallwas in their *Cultures in Conflict*, does indeed exist, and I find it unhelpful when people too quickly utter cries of persecution. I am not suggesting that Latter Day Saints didn't have some culpability for events in Missouri. But when the conflict ended, Latter Day Saints were imprisoned and prosecuted for their actions in northern Missouri while non-Latter Day Saints, including those involved in the murders at Haun's Mill, were not.

I will leave it to those with the credentials to do so to make the case, if one can be made, that Nauvoo makes far more sense when viewed through a lens as a deeply traumatized people. The classic symptom of post-traumatic stress disorder, if the movies are to be believed anyway, is the former soldier, home from war, diving for cover in response to unexpected noise.

Joseph Smith III describes just such an event in Nauvoo. Loren Walker, an aide to Joseph Smith Jr., had cleaned a brace of horse pistols and placed them on a canopy bed. A very young Joseph, waking from a nap, picked up one of the pistols, pulled the trigger of the weapon, and blasted a hole through the ceiling. Alarmed, a group of men holding a council in the neighboring room ran outside, sure that someone was making an attack on their president. Finding no one, they were puzzled, but Walker then remembered the pistols on the bed. They discovered little Joseph in the gunsmoke-filled canopy. The recoil had caused him to drop the gun on his own forehead with "a pretty sound thwack," resulting in a rapidly swelling bump—but with a worse injury to his nascent ego.[10]

From the Nauvoo Legion under Lieutenant-General Joseph to the overuse of habeas corpus to block-voting to the city ordinance allowing anyone trying to arrest Joseph to be imprisoned for life, the story of Nauvoo is, in so many ways, the story of a people reacting to the lingering traumas of Missouri.[11]

As Barbara Walden, Andrew Bolton, Ron Romig, and others have pointed out, Joseph Smith III witnessed the violence and its aftermath during these most difficult times and was shaped by these experiences. As a little boy at Far West he was separated from his father by the point of a Missouri militiaman's sword and would later

9. John E. Hallwas and Roger D. Launius, *Cultures in Conflict: A Documentary History of the Mormon War in Illinois* (Logan: Utah State University Press, 1995), 1–11.

10. Joseph Smith III, *The Memoirs of President Joseph Smith III, 1832–1914*, ed., Richard P. Howard (Independence, MO: Herald Publishing House, 2010), 25.

11. John S. Dinger, ed., *The Nauvoo City and High Council Minutes*, (Salt Lake City: Signature Books, 2011), 187–88.

be taken to visit his dad in the Liberty Jail.[12] Forced to leave his father behind when expelled from Missouri with his mother and siblings, Joseph lived temporarily near Quincy at the Cleveland farm where Emma repeatedly lectured him on the dangers of guns.[13] And later, during the summer and fall of 1842, nine-year-old Joseph III endured a number of searches of the family home in Nauvoo as sheriffs from Missouri looked for his father during repeated extradition attempts. He watched as his father and uncle left for Carthage, only to return in oak boxes and was present at the public viewing of their bodies. Hyrum was soon unrecognizable, and it was only through the burning of tar, vinegar, and sugar that it was bearable to be in the room.[14] Young Joseph was present during at least one re-interment of his father, and the coffin was opened to allow for a lock of hair to be snipped as a relic.[15] Following the outbreak of yet another violent conflict, he watched friends and family abandon Nauvoo to begin their epic trek west. And he himself would flee with his mother, brothers, and sister in September of 1846 as the battle of Nauvoo was about to break out, complete with artillery fire.[16]

Joseph III's memoirs, dictated over a period of five or six years during the "closing years of his life,"[17] (informed by his often sporadic diaries begun in 1859), offer us his take on some of these events and help us identify a few people who played a role in setting him on the path to peacemaker.

As a child, young Joseph had joined a "small troop of horsemen" and had learned how to use a foil under the direction of his uncle Arthur Millikin. When practicing one day, the weight of the foil caused his arm to drop, striking his horse's ear. The animal bolted and nearly ran away, generating considerable amusement among the other boys. Joseph commented, "had I been using a sword instead of a foil I would have deprived my mount of one of his ears."[18]

He soon graduated to drilling with "Bailey's boy troops," between four and six hundred strong, apparently an auxiliary of the Nauvoo Legion. As Joseph remembered it, "Though the organization [the Nauvoo Legion] continued for some time I drifted out of its younger portion, probably in deference to Mother's wishes."

Of the Legion itself, he said that it "helped to cultivate in the people a certain dependence upon human strength and power as a defense against the encroachments of their persecutors—perhaps a lamentable fact."[19] Joseph continued:

12. *The Memoirs of President Joseph Smith III*, 2–3.

13. Ibid., 4–5.

14. B. W. Richmond, "The Prophet's Death," *The Latter-day Saints' Millennial Star*, January 24, 1876, 52.

15. Ibid., 47.

16. Ibid., 39.

17. Ibid., 472.

18. Ibid., 25.

19. Ibid., 26.

> I have no desire or object, after the lapse of years, to sit in judgment or pass censure upon these men, though I may concede that I believe it was a mistake to allow the spirit of militarism to take possession of the leading authorities of the church to such an extent that in the reports of their movements there crept in the use of military appellations, such as lieutenant general, general, colonel, major, captain, to the exclusion of the ecclesiastical designations, such as president, high priest, apostle, elder, etc.
>
> Scripture was even cited as an excuse for such a departure from peaceful methods to maintain their rights—Israel under the law, Moses as a general, and Joshua and his comrades as warriors.
>
> Looking back along the pathway I feel it was a pity that such a spirit crept in among them, however, and a still greater one that the leading minds of the church partook of it.[20]

This statement is made even more significant by the fact that Joseph III was anything but quick to criticize his father.

Another event from the Nauvoo period that seemed to stand out to young Joseph involved bishop N. K. Whitney. As the church began to fragment following the death of Joseph Smith Jr., and as many made preparations for the trek west, several prominent Nauvoo citizens gave Joseph III gifts to remember them by. Brigham Young gifted the thirteen-year-old Joseph with a small pistol and George A. Smith, a large Bowie knife. Joseph offered the knife to his mother Emma for use in the kitchen. Apparently since he was quickly informed that Bowie knives don't have a place in the kitchen, he traded it instead with one of the Huntington boys for a large cherry rolling pin that he gave to his mother.

When Bishop Whitney heard of these gifts (the gun and the knife), he called Joseph to his home and presented him with his writing desk. Joseph remembered, "when Bishop Whitney gave me the desk he remarked that Elder Young and Cousin George A. had given me weapons of war, but he wished to impress upon me the sentiment that 'the pen is mightier than the sword.' I seemed to feel at the time that his intention was to foster within me a spirit of peace rather than one of conflict" and that "At all events these were the effects they produced upon me, for I did not imbibe the spirit of war, and had little use for its dangerous weapons."[21]

Another Nauvoo event that had made a life-long impression on Joseph involved Austin Cowles—a former member of the high council, a counselor in William Marks' Nauvoo Stake Presidency, and a later dissenter. Cowles had returned to Nauvoo, likely in the fall of 1845, and soon found himself surrounded by thirty young men and boys "whistling, and whittling towards him with wicked looking knives," and following him wherever he went throughout the day. Joseph saw Cowles about 4:00 p.m. as he headed toward the ferry to make his departure and spoke to him briefly.

20. Ibid., 24.

21. Ibid., 28–29.

On cue, "his escort struck up their din of whistling and whittling, hustling the poor old man with the ends of broken boards and the sticks they were whittling." Though thirteen-year-old Joseph attempted to stop the harassment, his intervention seemed only to intensify their efforts. He found it especially troubling that church members who had long complained of the "intolerance of bigotry" had themselves become bigots. The persecuted had become persecutors. Joseph wrapped up his story with a plea that God would "soon send the day when the curse of intolerance may be known no more in the land."[22]

Young Joseph was confronted with a number of issues related to peacemaking soon after affiliating with the Reorganization in 1860. One incident had roots in an event that took place about 1853. Emma Smith Bidamon, innkeeper at the Nauvoo Mansion House, took exception to the conduct of two boarders, one male and one female, and ordered them to move out. Insisting the woman should stay, the man drew a revolver and threatened Emma with it. Now really angry, Emma "firmly stated that both should go, and go at once." Joseph was away from home when the incident occurred but, upon learning of it when he returned, immediately "conceived a strong and inveterate hatred for the man." Emma's husband, quick-tempered Lewis Bidamon, was also away, but hearing the news on his return, grabbed a gun and set out to find the offender. But when Joseph next saw his stepfather, the latter was in a saloon having a drink with the man who had threatened his mother. This did nothing to relieve the hatred Joseph felt for the former boarder, a hatred that only increased through the years as he interacted with the man in several unrelated legal proceedings.

This became a significant problem for Joseph, especially after becoming a minister:

> I may say that when I began to preach the gospel I soon found I could not conscientiously use the words of the Lord's prayer-"and forgive us our trespasses as we forgive those who trespass against us"-without a twinge of conscience. Whenever I repeated them or even read them or thought of them, this hatred, which I had nursed for so long in my heart against the man who had abused my mother, would come to mind and accuse me.
>
> I finally saw that I must set myself to the task of overcoming this feeling, which I did humbly and earnestly. I am glad to say that, after a lapse of time, I was rewarded by the knowledge that the last vestige of my hate had disappeared and ill will was entirely banished ... The experience taught me a lesson. It forced upon my mind the necessity for many of the teachings of the Savior. I had a clearer understanding of what men were prone to feel of any unworthy nature and of the meaning of the prayer left for our example than I could have obtained had I not had this experience and learned to know what it was to hate a fellow-being. The knowledge helped to make me humble, and to

22. Edward William Tullidge, *Life of Joseph the Prophet* (Plano, IL: Board of Publication of the Reorganized Church of Jesus Christ of Latter Day Saints, 1880), 749–50.

> exercise sympathy and charity for others struggling under like feelings … Hatred is a cruel, destructive, and unlovely thing, and wholly unbecoming a Christian.[23]

Soon after assuming the presidency of the Reorganization, Joseph was confronted by the US Civil War. He attended a recruiting rally for the Union in the fall of 1861 at the Nauvoo City Hall. After several speeches were given, an officer called for volunteers. There was no response. Several of Nauvoo's German residents arrived fresh from the bar, including George Carmer, a friend of young Joseph's. Apparently as a prank, George and the others began calling out Joseph's name for a speech. The mayor soon took up the call as well and, despite his ragged overcoat, Joseph took the floor:

> I became imbued with the spirit of the occasion, and the fires of patriotism within me sprang into active flame. I made an impassioned appeal, moved by some inner light and urge which I did not stop to analyze, but the force of which I could not resist.
>
> Word got about that "Squire Smith" was speaking at the hall, and the room rapidly filled up … How long I addressed the people I do not now remember, but as I stopped, there was a rallying movement forward, and seventeen names were signed to the enlistment rolls … That was the first and only "war speech" I ever made.[24]

By 1863 when enlistments were not able to keep up with the North's need for troops, a draft was instituted, but one that allowed exemptions through substitution or payment of a fee. Much to the horror of Nauvoo's citizens, it was discovered that their township had not been given credit for their many previous volunteers since the war began. This became a problem when there were not enough able-bodied men left in the community to fill their quota. Frustrated by the failure to credit those already serving, Nauvoo residents began to raise money sufficient to hire substitutes.

Joseph Smith's 1832 prophecy regarding South Carolina and rebellion had heightened the interest of Joseph III and his brothers in the war considerably; they saw its outcome as either confirming or refuting their father's prophetic claims, and their ardent opposition to slavery pushed them towards involvement. According to young Joseph:

> As far as we were concerned, the question of becoming soldiers, either as volunteers or as under the draft, had involved, from the very beginning, many phases … As ordained ministers in a church whose rules of government and doctrine did not warrant the shedding of human blood except it became necessary in defense of our families or ourselves, we felt it should be contemplated only as a last resort. In spite of this firm conviction, our spirits stirred deeply to the call of patriotic duty. We laid the matter before our fellow church members, and the question was discussed in council meetings and in

---

23. *The Memoirs of President Joseph Smith III*, 126–27.

24. Ibid., 89.

> the general assemblies with much the same solemnity that doubtless characterized the Puritans, Quakers, Shakers, or other denominations whose tenets forbade the shedding of blood. Prayers' for guidance were fervently offered unto the Lord.
>
> When the answer came, it was clear, definite, and unmistakable ... In substance it was as follows: "Do not enlist. Enlisting makes your military service an individual and voluntary action, Whereby you will be responsible for the blood you might shed while in the service. Wait; if drafted, the responsibility is lifted. In such case do not hesitate to take your places in the ranks and to do your full duty as good soldiers and citizens, supporting the Government to the best of your powers. In such an event do not shirk any duty the service requires, even should it mean the shedding of human blood, for through the conscription the deed becomes a national sin instead of a personal one. The Nation as a whole will have to suffer for its sins, but you will not be held personally under moral obligations in the matter if you do not voluntarily enlist."[25]

Heeding this message, the Smith boys did not enlist, and according to Smith's later reminiscence, "We abided with calmness the outcome of the conscription draft later ordered." Alexander Hale Smith was eventually drafted, reported to Quincy as part of the "Nauvoo Squad," and was able to rejoin Joseph III two weeks later "in the walks of peace" when discharged as the result of an agreement between Iowa and Illinois officials giving each state credit for their citizens who had crossed the Mississippi to enlist. But when, not long after Alexander returned home, the agreement between the two states fell apart, the draft was once again on.[26]

Joseph's diary, recorded in shorthand as the events unfolded, presents a slightly less calm picture than the later reminiscence had. "At night I write to Bro. Rogers to tell him of the draft. What will he do with it? I am not prepared to say, but if I am drafted I expect that I will have to go to do my duty as a soldier or be treated as a deserter or coward. May I be preserved from so hard a fate, is my prayer to God."[27] Five days later he recorded, "Brother Derry is in trouble in regard to the draft, thinking of what will become of the wife and little ones [a family situation shared by Joseph III]. I am disturbed in my mind as well, but not to the extent that he is, yet. I am of the opinion that if God desires me to fight that I shall be protected by Him who so orders it."[28] He then cited the eighth chapter of Alma in the Book of Mormon. A week later Joseph served as secretary for a meeting of Nauvoo citizens trying to devise "ways and means to raise money to secure volunteers to fill the quota of said town upon the present call of 300,000 to be enforced by draft."[29] They were not successful.

---

25. Ibid., 90.

26. Ibid., 90–91.

27. Transcription of Joseph Smith III diary, 21 February 1865, Miscellany, P19, f31, Community of Christ Archives, Independence, Missouri.

28. Ibid., 26 February 1865.

29. Ibid., a longhand entry on the last page of the diary dated 4 March 1865.

On March 10, 1865, Joseph spent the day canvassing the flats, raising $108 to pay volunteers. Meeting with others working on the same task at the end of the day, he "found we were short of the required amount, so we rounded up our shoulders to take the draft. I see no way to avoid it. At the same time I should like to be able to do so if God were willing to permit me so to do."[30] Joseph spent the next three days focused on a church conference and then a day tending to his wife and young daughters, all sick, before recording "I feel reconciled to the draft, as I know I cannot help myself, so I intend to let it go as the Lord wills it to be."[31]

His last draft-related entry is found on March 15, 1865, "I hear no more about the draft, so I conclude that the citizens do not care much for it."[32] Reserving Joseph's later reminiscences for the rest of the story, lots were cast and a number of Nauvoo-area men were conscripted, including about five who were RLDS. The Smith boys were not among them. Much like Alexander's earlier experience, this group reported to Quincy, Illinois, and were soon discharged following Robert E. Lee's April 9, 1865 surrender at Appomattox.

Looking back on this exceptionally difficult time, Joseph reflected:

> Constantly I felt the duel impulse—the strong desire to enlist, and the equally strong reluctance when I contemplated the grave moral responsibility which would be placed upon me in case I did ... In writing this now, I do not intend to cast any reflection or place any blame upon any individual who did enlist, feeling it his duty to do so. A number of our brethren offered their services in that way, and were faithful under arms.[33]

As Joseph was struggling to balance his sense of patriotism with his understanding of the gospel, he was also working to rebuild a church presence in Nauvoo. Initially, the few RLDS members met in the home of Benjamin Austin and then the former home of William Marks on the corner of Water and Granger Streets. By 1864, the group had grown to seventy-five and moved into larger quarters across the street in the second floor of the Red Brick Store.[34] Joseph was chosen as pastor once the congregation was officially organized. As questions related to war and the draft swirled about, the name they chose was the "Olive Branch."[35]

Joseph's focus on the concept of peace would be expressed again through his role in the development of the first corporate seal for the Reorganization in 1874, though it would not be until many years later that it would become the widely used visual symbol of the church. He served with Jason Briggs and Elijah Banta on the three-

---

30. Ibid., 10 March 1865.

31. Ibid., 14 March 1865.

32. Ibid., 15 March 1865.

33. *The Memoirs of President Joseph Smith III*, 91.

34. *Life of Joseph the Prophet*, 782.

35. *The Memoirs of President Joseph Smith III*, 80.

member "committee on Church Seal" and submitted a design featuring a lion, lamb, and the motto "Peace."[36]

Another example of the increasing focus on peace in the church, perhaps in response to the Civil War, might well be the choice of "Lamoni," after a pacifist king in the Book of Mormon, for the name of an RLDS branch in Fayette Township, Decatur County, Iowa, in 1871. By the time the branch was established, the United Order of Enoch, a joint-stock company created by members of the Reorganization in 1870, had purchased 2,680 acres of land in the area on the way to a total of 3,300 acres. With the coming of the railroad, a town was officially platted in 1879, and Lamoni won out over Sedgwick, the previous post office, as the name of the new town.[37]

In 1893, Joseph represented the Reorganization at the Congress or Parliament of World Religions in Chicago. After being promised the opportunity to address the assembly in the main meeting hall, conference organizers reversed their position and offered leaders of "minor" religious bodies access only to a small room. Having spent days listening to leaders of larger denominations share their views, Joseph was quite annoyed by the reversal. Though it was left unsaid, he probably took some consolation in the fact that B. H. Roberts, representing the "Utah Mormon Church" and sitting just across the aisle and a few rows up, was also denied the use of the large hall. Both refused the opportunity to speak in the small room on principle.

One of the many speakers during the gathering, a "philosopher" from East India, made quite an impression on Joseph with his "arraignment" of western Christianity. He remembered the comments as "not made in ridicule nor malice" but "presented clearly and dispassionately, apparently the result of deep study, reflection, and reasoning." Joseph continued:

> I remember one statement he made: "You do not follow the teaching of the one you call 'Master,' for he commanded, 'If a man strike thee upon one cheek turn thou the other to him also.' You do not do this; you not only retaliate but are often the aggressors yourselves, and I nowhere can find in His instructions where you are commanded to strike anyone."

In what sounds like an endorsement of ecumenism, Joseph commented, "It impressed me as a pretty strong condemnation against the modern religious denominations who make great efforts to send their missionaries abroad for the purpose of proselytizing for what is called Christianity and yet, at the same time, have no

36. *True Latter Day Saints' Herald* 21 (May 1, 1874): 272. For more information on the development of the seal see Lawrence W. Tyree, "Impressions with a Purpose: Omissions, Myths, and the Real Origins of the Church Seal," *Restoration Studies* 12 (2011): 1–21.

37. Asa S. Cochran, "The Founding of Lamoni and the Work of the Order of Enoch," 130–131, 134 in *A History of Decatur County, Iowa and Its People*, vol. 1, ed. J. M. Howell and Heman C. Smith (Chicago: S. J. Clarke Publishing Company, 1915).

harmony or agreement among themselves, each presenting its own version of Christ and His message."[38]

In an 1894 *Saints' Herald* article, Joseph supported Christ's message of forgiveness and called his followers to do the same. He had received a letter of complaint stating that he (Joseph) had "joined hands with the persecutors of the Saints." His offense was saying "good morning" to an old man sitting in a wheelchair in the shade of the Carthage, Illinois, courthouse. The old man was Thomas C. Sharp, earlier public enemy number one for Latter Day Saints in Hancock County, Illinois. As editor of the *Warsaw Signal* newspaper, Sharp had called for the use of powder and ball to be rid of the Mormon problem and some evidence exists to suggest that he was one of the four who had shot Joseph Jr. In response to the complaint and others like it in which early members wanted to "cherish resentment" against those who had wronged them, Joseph III reminded the readers of the *Herald* that following Christ's example, they were required to forgive, that he (Joseph) forgave Thomas Sharp, and that any judgment to be made was the Lord's.[39]

The 1890s would also provide Joseph III the opportunity to revisit his earlier counsel to the church regarding enlistment and the draft as tension with Spain continued to build toward what would become the Spanish-American and Philippine-American Wars. Despite the call to wait to be drafted rather than to enlist, Joseph was quite sympathetic to those who surrendered to their sense of patriotic duty and volunteered to serve. This understanding extended even to members of his own family.

Apparently at the urging of his son Israel, who had already written his congressman to request consideration for a West Point appointment, Joseph wrote to Representative W. P. Hepburn on Israel's behalf. "My second son, Israel A. Smith, aged, 21, Feb. 22. last, desires an appointment to West Point ... will you take his name into consideration, and help him, if it strikes you favorably ... I think if he is appointed he will not disgrace the District"[40] (which sounds to me like a less-than-rousing endorsement). At twenty-one, Israel was "over the age at which admission is practicable,"[41] and he had to find an alternative path to service.

With the sinking of the USS Maine in February of 1898, the April 22 call by President McKinley for 125,000 volunteers to join the US National Guard, the dec-

38. *The Memoirs of President Joseph Smith III*, 319–20.

39. "Required to Forgive," *Saints' Herald* 41, no. 12 (March 21, 1894): 178–79. See page 277 of *The Memoirs of President Joseph Smith III* for evidence that Sharp pulled the trigger.

40. Joseph Smith III to Hon. W. P. Hepburn, 17 March 1897, P6 JSLB 7, 458–59. In his *Pragmatic Prophet: Joseph Smith III*, Roger Launius interprets this event as an attempt by Joseph to acquire an education for his younger son whom he could not afford to send to school. Since Israel had already written the congressman, my take is that Joseph is simply supporting his son's effort to gain the appointment.

41. Joseph Smith III to Hon. W. P. Hepburn, 31 March 1897, 475.

larations of war with Spain, and the April 27 opening of the US naval bombardment of Cuba, Israel couldn't resist trying again. He attempted to enlist in the National Guard on April 28, 1898 in Des Moines, but was rejected because of a bad left eye. Writing to his sister Audentia the same day he explained:

> I feel as if my duty to the United States has been fulfilled. I can feel now that I am under no obligation to answer the call for volunteers. I have offered my services to the US and been rejected ... soldering is not for me. I am afraid it is but another indication that perhaps my work is not to be with the world, but for it (Israel would become the 3rd prophet-president of the Reorganziation).
>
> But, should another call be made, I will answer, just as I did this time ... I feel very much disappointed. I could still try the regular army. But as I am not on the war path especially, I don't think I shall try it.[42]

Audentia shared her brother's letter with their father, and Joseph sent a note to his son a few days later. He was apparently either swept up in the same patriotic fervor as his son or was trying to raise his son's spirits following the rejection:

> I write to express my appreciation and approval of your action in offering yourself for service in the Army of the U.S.
>
> If there is any one thing on which I am at odds with some of the notions of the "unco guid," (a term for those who profess a strict morality) it is on the score of patriotism. "I am an American," and of the stock of Americans. There have been no cowards in the family so far back as I have traced it; and the love of country has been a ruling passion with them.
>
> I was of the opinion that you would offer, but was quite sure that your injured eye would disqualify you, especially at the opening of the hostilities.[43]

By October of 1899, Israel had moved to West Virginia, the focus of the war had shifted to the Philippines, and Joseph reminded his son of the position taken by the church since the 1860s:

> He who enlists in war is responsible for the blood he may shed; unless the fight be to repel invaders, or to defend his home. If the country engages in war and drafts men, then he who is drafted will not be held for the blood he sheds. So, while I feel your disability deeply, and would you were wholly sound physically, I can realize that it may be for the best that you have not the chance to lay your body down in disease in camp life or in the trenches where soldiers find their graves. It is honorable to stand in defence [*sic*] of American's institutions, but it is sadness and sorrow if men died in such defence [*sic*], to the home. I regret the war in the Philippines but can see no dodging it.[44]

---

42. Israel A Smith to Audentia Anderson, 28 April 1898, P13, f582, Community of Christ Archives.

43. Joseph Smith III to Israel A. Smith, 2 May 1898, P13, f583, Community of Christ Archives.

44. Joseph Smith III to Israel A. Smith, 3 October 1899, P13, f641, Community of Christ Archives.

After trying for three years and despite the words of counsel from his father, it appears that Israel finally successfully enlisted in the West Virginia National Guard in February of 1900. Joseph was supportive of the decision, pointing out to Israel that "It will not be to your disadvantage to train a little, learn the discipline and the tactics, manual of arms, and all that the situation permits."[45]

Joseph III understood the direction he perceived and shared on military service (don't enlist, but if drafted serve) in much the same way as his father understood the health code now known as the "Word of Wisdom," *viz*, "for the benefit of the ... church; ... not by commandment, or constraint."[46]

Second son Israel was something of a rebel. It couldn't have been easy growing up in the shadow of the heir apparent, his older brother Frederick M. Smith. Against the backdrop of international unrest and growing US and European interest in the cause of peace, Fred, on his own initiative, had attended The American Peace Society's National Peace Conference of 1910. The 1911 RLDS General Conference, presided over by Joseph Smith III, passed the following resolution:

> Whereas, we look with favor upon the growing sentiment throughout the civilized world in favor of peace and against war, and a resort to arbitration in both international and national disputes, and, Whereas, The Lord has commanded the church to "renounce war and proclaim peace," also to "lift up an ensign of peace and make a proclamation of peace unto the ends of the earth," therefore be it Resolved, That we, the ministry and delegates of the Reorganized Church of Jesus Christ of Latter Day Saints in conference assembled at Lamoni, Iowa, this 11th day of April, 1911, unreservedly commit ourselves to the conservation of world peace.[47]

The movement for world peace continued to build in the United States and in the church with apostles F. M. Sheehy and John W. Rushton attending the Fourth American Peace Congress in St. Louis, Missouri, in 1913 and reporting back to the 1914 General Conference:

> All who are interested in the abolition of the barbaric and costly method of war; of seeking to adjust international difficulties, whether politically, socially economically, or religiously inspired, join heartily and intelligently in seeking to solve these international questions by the arbitratment of justice and peace.[48]

Informed by his understanding of the Christian witness (section 95 of the Doctrine and Covenants that required a commandment to go to war), Joseph Smith III

45. Joseph Smith III to Israel A. Smith, 21 February 1900, P13, f656, Community of Christ Archives.

46. Doctrine and Covenants of the Church of the Latter Day Saints (Kirtland, OH: F.G. Williams and Co., 1835), section LXXX.

47. "Minutes of General Conference 1911," *Supplement to the Saints' Herald*, (1911) 1476.

48. "Minutes of General Conference 1914," *Supplement to the Saints' Herald*, (1914) 1915–16.

discouraged enlistment for military service while nevertheless encouraging service when conscripted. Joseph Smith III thus steered his followers towards peacemaking for fifty-one years. During the last years of his life, it must have been highly gratifying for Joseph to learn of the explosion of interest throughout the land in peacemaking and to hear prominent citizens declare that war would soon be extinct.[49] Of course the interest in peace was driven by growing instability in many parts of the world with Archduke Francis Ferdinand's assassination occurring during the final months of Joseph's life. The conflict that would grow into World War I had begun. The United Kingdom was fully engaged against Germany prior to Joseph's death on December 10, 1914, but the Unites States remained temporarily neutral, a position favored by Joseph III and other RLDS leaders until America's official entry into the conflict on April 6, 1917.

Not surprisingly, it was during times of war that the topic of peace was most often discussed, and it was during times of war that the church, its leaders and its members became transformed. Conflict in early Missouri had shifted the church from its pacifist leanings, and the 1838 Mormon War had created a traumatized people who reacted in Nauvoo in ways that often escalated tensions with its neighbors. Exposure to these events, combined with the moral and ethical questions generated by the US Civil War, redirected Joseph Smith III and his followers on a path to peace, a journey that would continue until the coming of World War I.

With the Civil War over but its horrors still fresh in the minds of many, Joseph III made his clearest statement on the centrality of peace to the mission of the church, making a link to section 95 of the Doctrine and Covenants and the requirement for a commandment from above before turning to violence:

> As to the principle of warlike Saints, when God commands me to fight, I shall do so, but not before; and I am strongly inclined to believe that he will not require me to fight. Whether God may, or may not, at some future day raise up a warlike people is a question open for dispute to those who may love discussion. But all are agreed that there is now no present commandment, and in the absence of the command Peace is eminently our mission. Hence my voice is for peace and let God take care of His own.[50]

An RLDS peace gene has been isolated, and it resides in the nucleus of Joseph Smith III.

---

49. F. Henry Edwards, *The History of the Reorganized Church of Jesus Christ of Latter Day Saints*, vol. 6, (Independence, MO: Herald Publishing House, 1970), 624.

50. Joseph Smith III to Samuel Powers, 25 April 1866, P13, f163, Community of Christ Archives.

Junctions & Communities

The Mormon History Association invites you to Ogden, Utah for its sixtieth annual conference to be held June 5-8, 2025. Situated on the Ogden and Weber Rivers near where they join the Great Salt Lake, and nicknamed "Junction City" when it became the connecting point between numerous railroad lines, Ogden has long been a site of junctions. Long before Latter-day Saints dreamed of an American Zion in the Great Basin, ancestors of Shoshone and other indigenous peoples criss-crossed the region, establishing trade networks and sharing languages, settlements, and cultures.

Ogden highlights a confluence of events and dynamics that shaped Mormon settlement, identity, and culture, and ensured that the tradition would always be intertwined with the wider world. The railroad especially brought diverse groups to Ogden. Wealthy investors and industrialists as well as Black Americans and Chinese, Japanese, German, and Irish immigrants were drawn to the burgeoning railroad town and its economic opportunities, bringing greater influence from the margins. They built communities that both constituted and contradicted centers of Latter-day Saint power, resulting in diversity, and alternative directions. Conversely, families like Apostle Franklin D. and Jane S. Richards represented Ogden's influence on the highest levels of the church.

In the 20th century, international and national events continued to encourage convergence at Ogden. World War II brought a military base, prisoner of war camps, and defense industries. Later immigration trends further heightened the diverse influences and people that would shape Utah and today's global church. Influenced by outside elements, Ogden's Mormon community continued to develop a unique religious and cultural brand that included diverse politics and a cultural presence perhaps best represented by the Osmonds, as well as iconic Mormon composer Janice Kapp Perry. Ogden also produced several prominent western historians including Fawn Brodie, Bernard Devoto, and more recently Thomas Alexander, a founding member of MHA.

While distance and distinction from others are popular tropes in the telling of Mormon histories, gathering in "Junction City" invites us to widen the lens and remember the many histories of interaction and influence that have shaped and been shaped by Restoration traditions. Ogden's Union Station embodies the variety of these historical junctures, sitting as it does at the intersection of Wall Avenue's business world and 25th Street's demimonde history.

Our 2025 theme,"Conjunctions and Communities," invites presentations that explore the Restoration movement as a hub of internally intersecting variation with a history long enmeshed in broader worlds, contexts, and contingencies. We encourage scholars to reconsider points of convergence in the Latter-day Saint past, to explore coalitions and crossroads, and to be open to approaches that creatively join methodologies and fields.The deadline for proposals is November 1, 2024. Submit your proposal to the program co-chairs through the Google form accessible via the MHA homepage. Questions may be sent to the program committee co-chairs at mhaogden2025@mormonhistoryassociation.org. Notifications for acceptanceand rejections will be sent by January 17, 2025. For additional information about the conference,please visit mormonhistoryassociation.org.

JWHA 2025 CALL FOR PAPERS

Politics and Religion: The Impact of Governance and Government on the Restoration Movements from 1830 to the Present

2025 Annual Conference
Independence, Missouri
September 18–21, 2025

Our conference in 2025 falls on the centennial anniversary of debates about supreme directional control in the RLDS church and the "Scopes Monkey Trial" on the national level. We will also be meeting at the Harry S. Truman Presidential Library and Museum in Independence, Missouri, at the heart of a landscape where tensions between politics and religion have had a lasting impact on the community. Papers might include church leaders' interactions with US presidents, reactions to Supreme Court rulings, social justice issues, attitudes toward scientific developments, the role of religion in education, political demographics of Restoration religions, institutional statements of party advocacy or neutrality, and more. With politics on everyone's mind these days, there will be plenty to debate!

We look forward to hearing about your historical research either with individual papers or as part of a panel discussion. We also encourage theological papers related to our Restoration Studies track. Please submit your one hundred to two hundred-word proposals by April 6, 2025, to proposals@jwha.info.

Walking Tours

Friday, September 13
5:00 – 7:00 p.m.
Preregistration Required

Downtown St. George

Guides: Loren Webb, Washington County Historical Society & Reuben Wadsworth

From the Dixie Center Convention Center parking lot, drive 2.9 miles north on Main Street to the Ancestor Square parking lot, about 140 North Main. The parking lot will be on the west or left side of the road. The parking lot can also be accessed from about 140 North 100 West and from about 75 West 200 North. Parking is free.

All tour participants head east to the sidewalk on Main Street, then turn south to meet at the northwest corner of St. George Boulevard and Main Street. Both tours will begin and end in front of the south entrance of George's Restaurant, 2 West St. George Blvd.

Tour participants have been divided into two groups, check your name tag for your group number.

Note: To take advantage of an inside tour of the Brigham Young Winter Home conducted by the Church of Jesus Christ of Latter-day Saints missionaries, both group tours will begin promptly at 5 p.m. and end at 7 p.m. Brigham Young Winter Home tours end at 6 p.m.

The first half of the WCHS conducted tour is called the Ancestor Square Block Tour, and will feature historic information about the *Big Hand Cafe* (now the site of *George's Corner Restaurant*), which was the center of town, the *Morris-Grundy home*, the *Samuel and Esther Miles Jr.* home, the *St. George Opera House* (located northeast from the 200 North roundabout), the *Brigham Young Winter Home*, the *Edwin and Mary Woolley Foster home* (now Mulberry Inn), the *Dr. Israel and Anna Ivins home* (first St. George physician), *Anthony and Elizabeth Ivins home* (Anthony Ivins became an LDS apostle and member of the First Presidency during the Heber J. Grant presidency), the *Gardner Club Hall* (one of the oldest public buildings still in use in St. George) and the *Augustus and Elizabeth Hardy home* (Augustus was one of the early sheriffs in the county).

To access the second half of the tour, called the Green Gate Village Block Tour, participants will need to cross from the north to the south side of St. George Boulevard at the intersection of Main and St. George Boulevard at a pedestrian crosswalk.

Highlights of the Green Gate Village Block Tour includes reference to the *St. George Cooperative Mercantile Building* (now Bear Paw Cafe), the *Wadsworth Building which once housed the Dixie Theater and now houses Gallery 35*, an art studio, the *Bishop's Storehouse*, now a real estate office, and *Green Gate Village* which includes *Judd's Store*, the oldest business in St. George, along with the *Orson Pratt/Richard and Elizabeth Bentley home* (now housing a clothing store), and several other homes which were moved to the Green Gate Village by former owners Mark and Barbara Greene.

Also visible from the southeast corner of the Green Gate Village Block Tour is the historic *LDS Tabernacle*, across the street to the south, and the historic *Woodward School Building* to the west, across the street to the south at 100 West and Tabernacle.

The length of this tour is 4 blocks or about a half mile in length. Elevation changes on this block or less noticeable.

The total length of the overall tour would be about 8.5 blocks or 1.5 miles including walking to and from the Ancestor Square parking lot.

Both tours will last two hours.

Juanita Brooks Property

Carpooling is Recommended

Guides: Brooks Family Members

The starting address for the Brooks tour will be 356 N Main Street where you will be divided into groups.

There is street parking on both sides of the street, ten to fifteen car potential, but carpooling will be essential. There is also parking at the Brooks nature park one block or 1/4 mile north of the house, some, depending on number of participants, will start there. There is also parking at the bottom of the hill at the St George Art Museum, 47 E 200 N, and the Eye Care Center across the street (which will be closed by the time we start) at 10 Diagonal St. From the last two locations, walk up the hill.

Participants will be divided into groups to move in a clockwise rotation through the five properties. Each guide will present the same script.

Post Tour Dining Options

Looking for a place to eat in the downtown area following the tour? There are some limited options:

Pizza Factory, 2 West St. George Blvd. Suite 8, Monday through Saturday, 11 a.m. to 9 p.m.

George's Restaurant, 2 West St. George Blvd., Friday and Saturday, 8 a.m. to 11 p.m. or later.

Paleta's Gourmet Creamsicles, 73 N. Main, Monday through Saturday, 12 p.m. to 10 p.m.

Pica Rica American Barbecue, 25 N. Main, Friday, 11 a.m. to 8 p.m.

Bombay Cafe, (curry and grill express), 40 West Tabernacle, Monday through Saturday, 4:30 p.m. to 9:30 p.m.

Twisted Noodle Healthy Eats, 20 North Main, Suite 108, Friday, 7:30 a.m. to 8 p.m.

Iceberg Drive-in, 222 East St. George Boulevard, Friday, 10:30 a.m. to 12 midnight. (This location is 2 blocks farther east of the downtown historic district).

Sunday Hymn Fest

St. George Tabernacle
18 S Main Street, St. George, UT 84770

Driving Directions:

From the Dixie Center, head south and turn right onto 120 East. Go 1/10 of a mile to Dixie Drive and get onto I-15 headed north. Go a half mile and take the right fork on UT-18N/Bluff St. get off the freeway and turn right onto Main Street, St. George. Keep on Main until getting to 18 South. It's the tall red brick building that is visible from a great distance away.

Hymn Festival

John Whitmer Historical Association

Sunday, September 15, 2024
St. George, Utah

WELCOME: Mark Staker

Organist: Mike Karpowitz
Chorister: Brian Hales

Opening Song

1. Guide Us O Though Great Jehovah (1835 Hymnal #13)

OPENING PRAYER

Utah Latter-day Saint Church

2. Where Can I Turn for Peace
3. Come, Come, Ye Saints

James J. Strang Tradition:

4. The Prophet J. J. Strang
5. The City of Voree

Church of Jesus Christ—Bickerton Tradition

6. Sing Glory!

Fundamentalist Mormon Tradition

7. O My Mother
8. Redeemer Mine

Community of Christ with John Hamer and Mike Karpowitz

9. God Has Spoken in All Ages
10. Is There One Who Feels Unworthy?
11. We're Marching to Zion

1835 Hymnal:

12. The Spirit of God

CLOSING PRAYER

No. 51. Guide Us, O Thou Great Jehovah

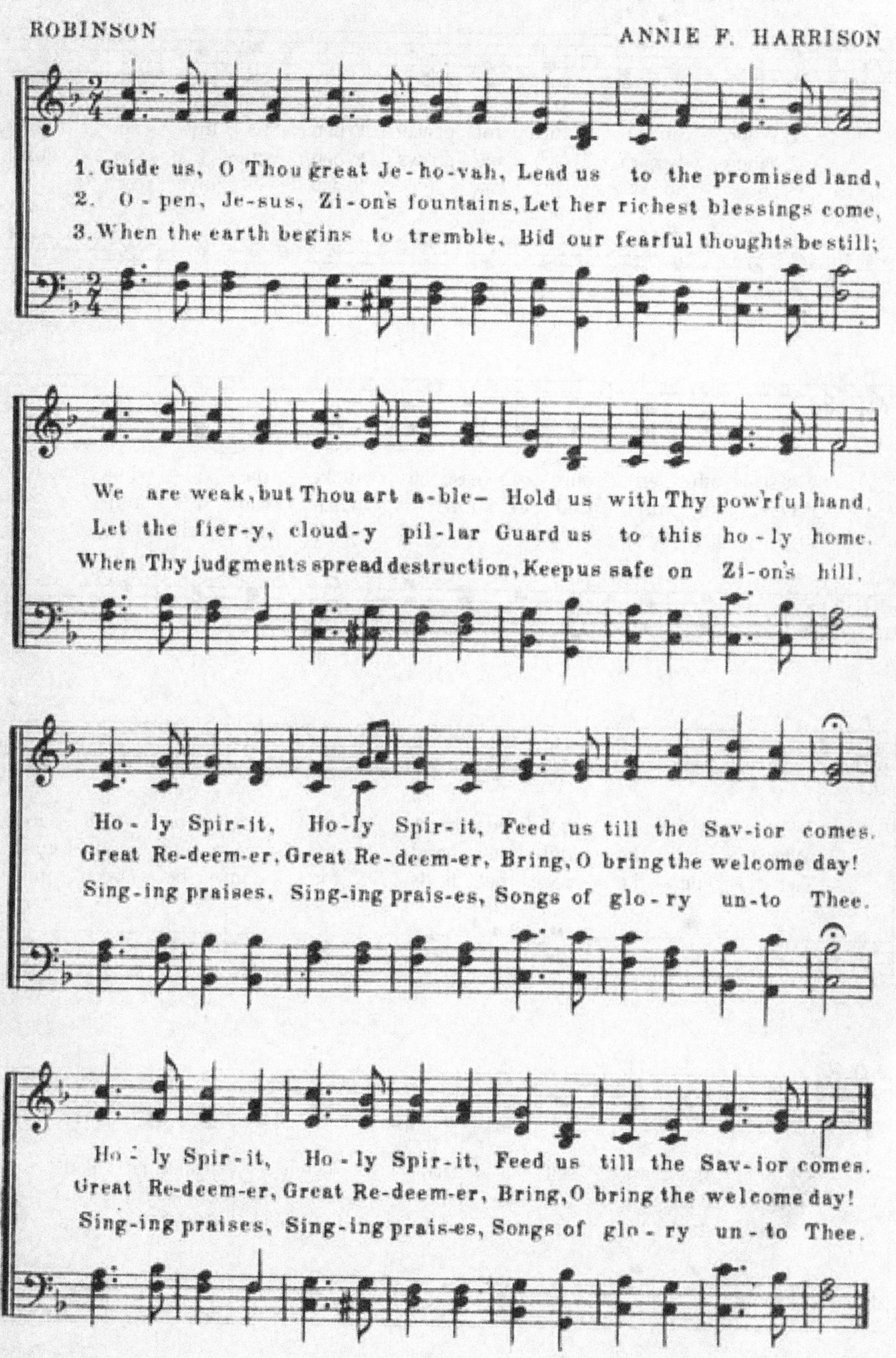

Where Can I Turn for Peace?

Text: Emma Lou Thayne, b. 1924. © 1973 IRI
Music: Joleen G. Meredith, b. 1935. © 1973 IRI

John 14:27; 16:33
Hebrews 4:14–16

Come, Come, Ye Saints

The Prophet J. J. Strang

Text: Charles B. Thompson

The City of Voree

By William B. Smith, (Joseph Smith's brother)

To the tune of "A Poor Wayfaring Man of Grief"

The original song had twenty-one verses.

146. SING GLORY!

(Psalm 96:1 "O Sing unto the Lord a new song: sing unto the Lord, all the earth.")

Arranged by Eugene F. Amormino

Words and Music by Arlene L. Buffington

* sing notes on last ending

Music may be interchanged with "O My Father."
This was Brother Brigham's favorite tune for "O My Father."

170 Redeemer Mine

Rulon C. Allred

Ethelbert Nevin arr.

Redeemer Mine

God Has Spoken in All Ages

2

God, whose works are nev - er end - ed, and whose words shall
for the In - fi - nite is broad - er than our minds can
As our in - tel - lect in - creas - es, as our spir - its
Ne - phites, Jews, all scat - tered Is - rael shall each oth - er's

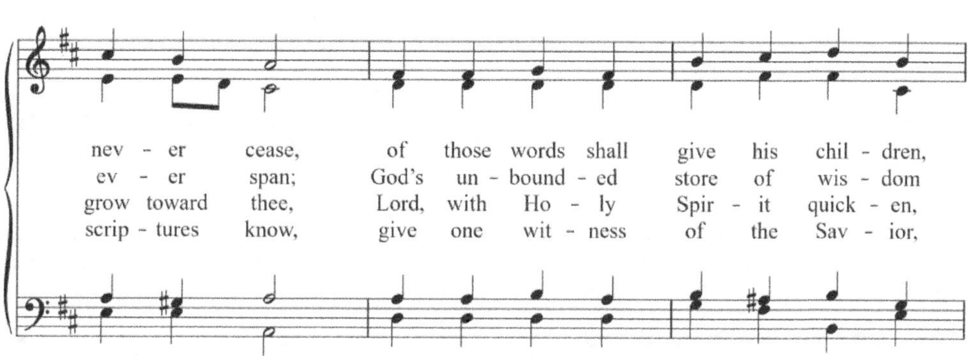
nev - er cease, of those words shall give his chil - dren,
ev - er span; God's un - bound - ed store of wis - dom
grow toward thee, Lord, with Ho - ly Spir - it quick - en,
scrip - tures know, give one wit - ness of the Sav - ior,

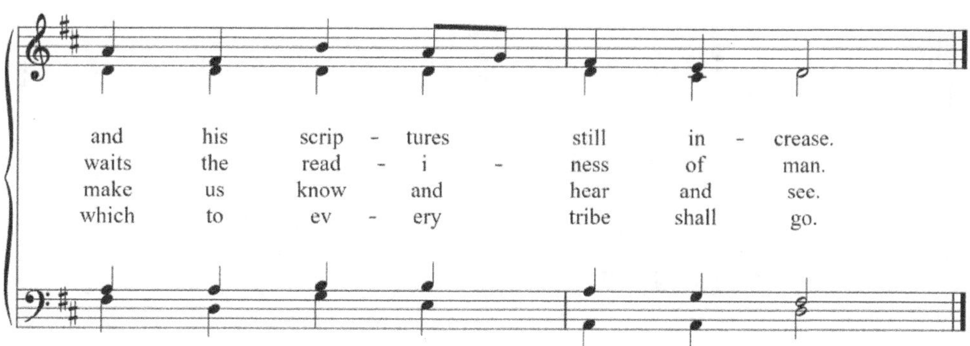
and his scrip - tures still in - crease.
waits the read - i - ness of man.
make us know and hear and see.
which to ev - ery tribe shall go.

Is There One Who Feels Unworthy?

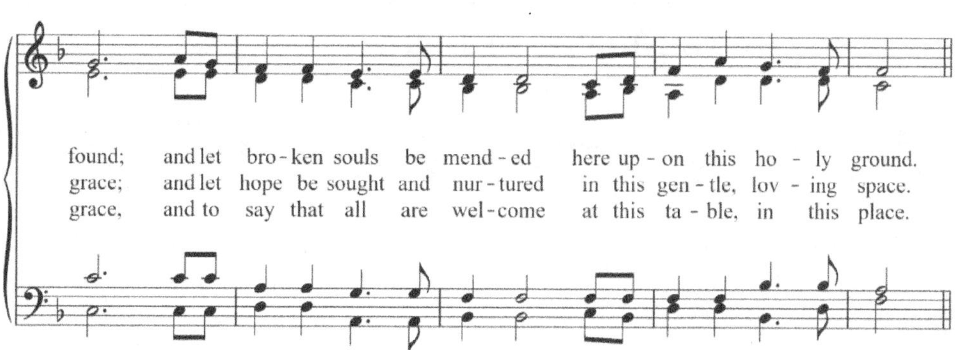
found; and let bro - ken souls be mend - ed here up - on this ho - ly ground.
grace; and let hope be sought and nur - tured in this gen - tle, lov - ing space.
grace, and to say that all are wel - come at this ta - ble, in this place.

Here in this ho - ly place, here in this
Here in this ho - ly place, here in this gen - tle

gen - tle space, there is no lack of grace, here in this ho - ly place.
space, there is no lack of grace, here in this ho - ly place.

We're Marching to Zion (Verse 1)
God's Melody of Peace (Verses 2 & 3)

2
Refrain
We're march - ing to Zi - on, beau - ti-ful, beau - ti-ful Zi - on; we're
We're sing - ing a new song, lyr - ics of love in a tune strong. We're
We're sing - ing a new song, lyr - ics of love in a tune strong. We're
march - ing up-ward to Zi - on, the beau - ti-ful ci - ty of God.
called to sing out a peace song, with hope, to cre - ate a new world.
called to sing out a peace song, with hope, to cre - ate a new world.

33 The Spirit of God Like a Fire Is Burning

III Nephi 8:25, 26
D. and C. 85:18

PARACLETE 12.11.12.11. with refrain

1. The Spir - it of God like a fire is burn - ing;
2. The Lord is ex - tend - ing his saints' un - der - stand - ing,
3. We call in our sol - emn as - sem - blies, in spir - it,

The lat - ter - day glo - ry be - gins to come forth;
Re - stor - ing their judg - es and all as at first;
To spread forth the king - dom of heav - en a - broad,

The vi - sions and bless - ings of old are re - turn - ing;
The knowl - edge and pow - er of God are ex - pand - ing;
That we through our faith may be - gin to in - her - it

The an - gels are com - ing to vis - it the earth.
The veil o'er the earth is be - gin - ning to burst.
The vi - sions and bless - ings and glo - ries of God.

Text: W. W. Phelps, 1792-1872.
Tune: English Tune.

Sung at the dedication of Kirtland Temple.

Made in the USA
Middletown, DE
04 September 2024